EZEKIEL & DANIEL
A SELF-STUDY GUIDE

Irving L. Jensen

MOODY PRESS
CHICAGO

©1968 by
THE MOODY BIBLE INSTITUTE
OF CHICAGO

Moody Press Revised Edition, 1990

Scripture quotations, unless noted otherwise, are taken from the King James Version.

The use of selected references from various versions of the Bible in this publication does not necessarily imply publisher endorsement of the versions in their entirety.

ISBN: 0-8024-4458-X

2 3 4 5 6 Printing/EP/Year 94 93 92 91

Printed in the United States of America

Contents

Introduction

Of the four major prophets (Isaiah, Jeremiah, Ezekiel, Daniel), Ezekiel and Daniel give the most attention to end-time events of world history scheduled on God's timetable. These two men were prophets living in exile, which partly explains why so many predictions of latter days appear in their writings. The big questions in their day, as the end of the seventy-year captivity period approached, were: What is *next* in store for Israel? Is there any hope of restoration? If so, when will it come? In answering these questions, God showed Ezekiel and Daniel that there was much tribulation for Israel in the centuries to come, but that He would always preserve a believing remnant. God also revealed that in the consummation of world history, Israel would finally look to the Messiah and worship Him as the rightful King on the throne of David.

The day of Christ's coronation cannot be far distant. Surely it behooves us as people of God and lovers of His Word to know what He wrote about these last days through His prophets Ezekiel and Daniel. It is the purpose of this manual to help the reader make a serious, diligent study of these important prophecies.

A main reason that a book of prophecy may be difficult to understand is that the person reading it is not acquainted with the various aspects of the background of the book, such as its historical setting. In an earlier manual, *Isaiah and Jeremiah*, I included a chapter on Old Testament prophecy in general. The reading of that chapter will give introductory help to the student of this manual on Ezekiel and Daniel as well.

Many charts and diagrams have been included in this study book, to help the reader see the *whole* picture of the subject being studied in relation to the *parts*. The analytical chart method of study is used at times in the analysis of the biblical text.

Relate the teachings to your personal life

As you approach the books of Ezekiel and Daniel, remember that *you* are the student of these biblical writings. Do not be content with merely being told what the text says or means. Reflect on what is involved in the following areas, concering *you*:

1. *Your purposes:*
    Why are you studying these books?
    Define your goals first; then pursue them diligently.
2. *Your attitudes:*
    How important these are!
    Do you *want* to learn?
    Do you lean on the Spirit for His enlightenment in your studies?
    Are you willing to spend much time and effort in Bible study?
3. *Your methods:*
    Success in Bible study depends much on *how* you study.
    Methods vary according to the student's background, previous instruction, and native abilities. Various methods of study are suggested in this manual. But however you study, be sure you LOOK—LOOK—LOOK (observation), and JOT IT DOWN (recording). These are musts in effective Bible study.
4. *Your applications:*
    These reflect the purposes of your study. This manual will not always ask for an application, but it should be one of your good habits always to apply the passage to your own life, as well as to the world in which you live. Remember, all Scripture is profitable!

Lesson 1
The Man Ezekiel

When God began to send His people into captivity for their sin, that did not mean He would no longer speak to them. If God was to purge the nation of their corrupt idolatry, they needed to hear more of the very word they had so stubbornly resisted. Among the Jews taken captive by King Nebuchadnezzar of Babylon in his second invasion of Judah in 597 B.C. was a man by the name of Ezekiel. This was the one whom God chose to be His *prophet to the exiles*, while Daniel served as God's *ambassador to the court* of the captor king.

In this lesson we shall study about the *man* Ezekiel. This will serve as helpful background for the following lesson, which is a survey study of the *book* of Ezekiel. From that point the lessons will be devoted to detailed analyses of various passages of Ezekiel.

I. EZEKIEL AND HIS CONTEMPORARIES

The Bible cannot be charged with needless duplication. Whenever there is duplication, it is with divine purpose. The ministry of Ezekiel is an example of this. Much of what Ezekiel preached was very similar to Jeremiah's preaching, which the former prophet must have listened to often in Jerusalem, up until his exile at age twenty-five.[1] And yet the two prophets were very different from each other, partly in what they said and partly in the setting of their ministries. Concerning the latter, study Chart A, titled "Ezekiel and His Contemporaries." (Refer also to Chart Z.) The main thing to

1. Jeremiah may have been as much as twenty years older than Ezekiel. Ezekiel and Daniel were about the same age. Concerning Ezekiel's familiarity with Jeremiah's message it has been said that Ezekiel was "the prolongation of the voice of Jeremiah." The two prophets were brought into juxtaposition especially in connection with Jeremiah's letter to the exiles, to whom Ezekiel was ministering. (Read Jer. 29.)

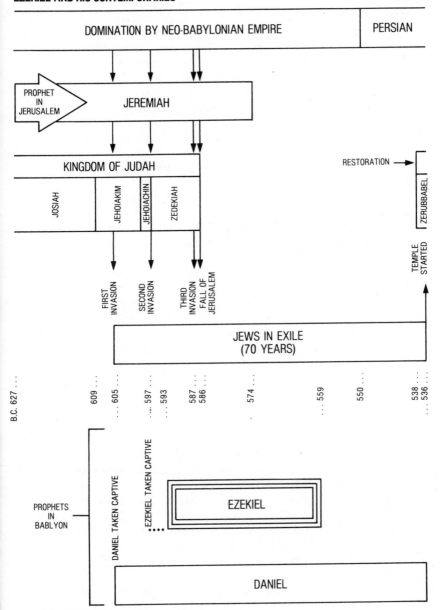

observe on Chart A is that both Daniel and Ezekiel did not begin their prophetic ministries until they were deported to Babylonia. Daniel was taken captive in 605 B.C., in Nebuchadnezzar's first invasion of Jerusalem, and began his prophetic ministry in that same year. (Read Dan. 1:1-7.) Ezekiel was deported to Babylon in 597 B.C. along with King Jehoiachin and hosts of citizens, when Nebuchadnezzar invaded Jerusalem the second time. (Read 2 Kings 24:10-16.) Ezekiel was not called to prophesy until after he had been in Babylonia for about five years. Thus Jeremiah was the lone prophet in the land of Judah for the last twenty years before Jerusalem's fall; Daniel and Ezekiel served as prophets only in captivity.

The different ministries of the three contemporaneous prophets may be identified thus:

1. Jeremiah: prophet mainly to the Jews in Jerusalem, before the city fell.

2. Daniel: prophet mainly to the court of King Nebuchadnezzar, in Babylonia.

3. Ezekiel: prophet mainly to the exiles in Babylonia, before and after the fall of Jerusalem. Ezekiel was *the* prophet of the captivity.

It is interesting that in Ezekiel's book there is no mention of Jeremiah, whereas Daniel is mentioned three times (Ezek. 14:14, 20; 28:3). Daniel, because of his favor at the king's court, was well known throughout Babylonia by the time Ezekiel arrived in the country. Daniel's prophecy refers to Jeremiah once (Dan. 9:2), and the name Ezekiel does not appear in either of the other two books.

II. THE TIMES IN WHICH EZEKIEL LIVED

The idolatry that Ezekiel saw as Judah's blight before he left Jerusalem was the same condition he faced in the settlements of Jewish exiles in Babylonia. The judgment of captivity did not stir the first contingents of exiles to repentance. In fact they found it very hard to believe, as Ezekiel was prophesying, that Jerusalem would actually be destroyed by the Babylonians. They were loath to believe that Jehovah had given world dominion to Babylon, and that His will was for Judah to submit to this enemy. Hence it was necessary for Ezekiel in Babylon—and Jeremiah in Jerusalem—to show the people how unfounded were any expectations of immediate deliverance.

This, of course, was not a message the people liked to hear. A small minority responded, but for the most part the people would

8

not believe the prophet's words. They succumbed to the evil influences that surrounded them and lost faith in the covenant promises of Jehovah. Then, too, the presence of the false prophets (some of whom had been brought to Babylon in the first two captivities) made the ministry of Ezekiel difficult, because they were contradicting all that Ezekiel preached. Ezekiel told the Jews they had better settle down and make homes in Babylon, because the bondage would last seventy years. But the false prophets insisted that this captivity was only temporary and that they would soon be back in their own land.

III. EZEKIEL'S PERSONAL HISTORY

Of Ezekiel's personal history we are told very little. However, enough information may be garnered from various Bible references to project a biographical profile of this fascinating prophet.

A. Name

The name Ezekiel is written in Hebrew as *Yehezqel*, meaning "God strengthens." The prophet was truly a tower of strength in the midst of a defeated people. Also God made him strong to resist the opposition of hardhearted and rebellious Israelites (read 3:8-9).

B. Birth

If the phrase "thirtieth year" of 1:1 refers to Ezekiel's age at that time (593 B.C.), then he was born in 623 B.C., during the reign of good King Josiah. Ezekiel was a mere child when the book of the law was recovered in the course of renovating the Temple in 621 B.C. The years of his boyhood and youth were thus spent in the bright reformation period that followed that recovery.

C. Family

Ezekiel, like Jeremiah, was born of a priestly heritage. His father's name was Buzi, a priest possibly of the Zadok line (1:3; 40:46; 44:15). Ezekiel was married, but it is not known if he had any children. The darkest day of his life was when the Lord announced to him two tragic events: the siege of Jerusalem (24:2) and the death of his beloved wife (24:15-18).

D. In Exile

When Ezekiel was about eighteen years old (605 B.C.) the Babylonians (also known as Chaldeans) made their first invasion into Judea, carrying away some captives, among whom was Daniel (see Chart Y). Eight years later (597 B.C.) they came again, and this time Ezekiel was among the captives, who constituted the upper classes of Judah. Read 2 Kings 24:10-17 for the historical record of this (cf. Ezek. 1:2; 33:21). Some of the exiles were incarcerated; others were made slaves; many were allowed to settle down in their own homes in various settlements of the exiles (cf. Jer. 29:1-7; Ezra 2:59; Neh. 7:61). It was of divine providence that Ezekiel was among those granted such liberties. His home was in Tel-abib (3:15), a principal colony of exiles near the fabulous city of Babylon. Tel-abib was located by the canal Chebar ("Grand Canal"), which flowed "from the Euphrates fork above Babylon through Nippur, winding back into the Euphrates near Erech"[2] (cf. 1:1, 3; Ps. 137:1).

Ezekiel's home was a meeting place where the elders of the Jews often came to consult him (8:1; 14:1; 20:1). It may be that his home was open to any of the exiles who wanted spiritual help.

E. Call and Commission

Five years after his arrival in the strange land of Babylon, Ezekiel received his call to the prophetic office, to minister to the exiles in Babylonia.[3] What he experienced and heard in this call is recorded in the first three chapters of his book.

Like the other prophets, Ezekiel received a vision of God that put him on his face in the dust before his Maker (1:26-28). Compare Isaiah's vision (Isa. 6) and John's vision (Rev. 1:10-18). Observe that in each instance it was the Lord Jesus Christ who was seen, and that each vision produced the same humbling effect upon the beholder. Compare the three visions, and observe the different ways in which the Lord manifested Himself. To Isaiah, His *holiness* was emphasized; to Ezekiel, His *power*, majesty, and government; and to John, His *love*. Concerning this, someone has written, "How surpassingly blessed, that this infinitely holy, all-powerful One loves us so that He will come down among us and teach us!"

2. Merrill F. Unger, *Unger's Bible Handbook* (Chicago: Moody, 1966), p. 364.
3. His activities during this five-year period are not chronicled for us, but we may assume that he ministered to his people's spiritual needs and did much studying of the law and the prophetical writings. God was preparing the priest to be the prophet during these years.

Twenty-two years later (see 29:17), when Ezekiel was around fifty-two years old, he was still prophesying to the exiles. It is not known how much longer his ministry continued.

IV. EZEKIEL'S CHARACTER

Ezekiel the prophet was strong and fearless. This is what God made him (3:8-9), and this was his dominant characteristic. He had boundless energy and a love for the simple, clear, and direct. Though his disposition was firm, he had a shepherd's heart for his countrymen. "Ezekiel is the one who, in the first place, breaking in pieces the hard hearts with the hammer of the law, represents the strict inexorable judge, but therefore, pouring soothing balm into the open wounds, approves himself as the healing physician."[4]

Ezekiel's book reveals that he was methodical, artistic, and mystic. With a deeply introspective nature, he must have studied much the message of God as it applied to himself and his brethren. He was truly a practical theologian, and for this he has been called "the first dogmatist of the Old Testament" and "the prophet of personal responsibility."

V. EZEKIEL THE PROPHET, PRIEST, AND PASTOR

Ezekiel's ministry combined the labors of prophet, priest, and pastor.

A. Prophet

He was a seer to whom God gave many visions concerning the present and future. He was God's spokesman to the people, powerfully preaching against sin and challenging them to turn from idolatry to God.

B. Priest

Ezekiel was also God's priest. God said regarding the exiled Jews, "Although I have cast them far off among the heathen, and although I have scattered them among the countries, yet will I be to them as a little sanctuary in the countries where they shall come" (11:16). And so God gave Ezekiel to them to serve like a priest in this "sanctuary," a channel of communication between themselves and the God they had so shamefully dishonored.

4. *Calwer Handbuch* as cited by John Peter Lange, "Ezekiel," *Commentary on the Holy Scriptures,* reprint ed. (Grand Rapids: Zondervan, n.d.), p. 2.

C. Pastor

The turning point of Ezekiel's ministry was the fall of Jerusalem, in 586 B.C. For the seven years prior to this (593-586 B.C.), he preached mostly of repentance and judgment (chaps. 1-24). Now, with their city destroyed—even as Ezekiel had predicted—the people found themselves in the valley of despair. This turned out to their advantage, however, for now they would begin to listen to Ezekiel, whose new message was one of consolation—the future restoration of Israel (chaps. 33-48). Little by little the people responded, turning from their idolatrous ways, led by their pastor Ezekiel. Ezekiel was their "consoler, a herald of salvation, an expositor of the necessity of inner religion, a prophet of the regathering, and the envisager of God's restoration of the Temple, worship, and land to a redeemed and purified Israel (33:11; 34; 36:25-31; 37; 40-48)."[5]

VI. EZEKIEL'S MESSAGE

Ezekiel's message was geared to the circumstances and needs of his audience. Keep in mind the historical setting that this lesson has been describing, and you will understand why these were his major points:

A. Sin Caused Exile

It was sin that brought the people's judgment of exile. The people must repent and return to God.

B. Seventy-Year Exile

The exile would last for seventy years, even though false prophets were preaching an early return. The people had a letter from Jeremiah (Jer. 29), which concurred with Ezekiel's preaching. The seventy-year captivity began in 605 B.C. with the first deportation of Jews (Jer. 25:11-12; Zech. 7:5). Before the Jews could return to Jerusalem, they must return to the Lord.

C. Future Restoration

There would be a future restoration of Israel for a believing remnant. The general impression of these consolatory messages was

5. Charles F. Pfeiffer and Everett F. Harrison, eds. *The Wycliffe Bible Commentary* (Chicago: Moody, 1962), p. 704.

that this restoration was in the far-distant future. Most of the adults of Ezekiel's audience had no other hope than this, for seventy years of captivity precluded their returning to Jerusalem in their lifetime.

The tone of Ezekiel's preaching was austere and impressive, for the prophet constantly stressed the sovereignty and glory of the Lord. The phrase "glory of the Lord" or its equivalent appears eleven times in the first eleven chapters of his book. The statement of God "They shall know that I am the Lord" or its equivalent appears about seventy times in the book. A comparison of the main themes of the four "greater prophets" is shown here:

Isaiah: salvation of the Lord
Jeremiah: judgment of the Lord
Daniel: kingdom of the Lord
Ezekiel: sovereignty and glory of the Lord

The captivity of Israel and Judah was God's judgment for their idolatry. It was during the captivity years that some of the people returned to God. This was the beginning of the religion of Judaism, and because Ezekiel was the prominent prophet at this time, he has been called "the father of Judaism."

Questions on Lesson 1

1. Who were Ezekiel's contemporaries, and in what capacities did they serve?

Jeremiah

Daniel

2. Describe what you can recall about Ezekiel's name, birth, family, exile, and call.

3. Describe Ezekiel's personality.

_____

_____

_____

4. Compare the ministries of Jeremiah, Ezekiel, and Daniel.

_____

_____

_____

5. Compare the divine calls of Ezekiel, Isaiah, and the apostle John.

_____

_____

_____

6. What were the three main themes of Ezekiel's message to the Jews in exile?

_____

_____

_____

Lesson 2
The Book of Ezekiel

The book of Ezekiel records its author's biography and the history of the time when he lived and worked. Our study now converges on the *text* of this book in which Ezekiel's biography and history have been recorded for all ages. Our ultimate goal will be to derive spiritual lessons from the book that are applicable today.

I. STYLE OF EZEKIEL

Although it is true that most of the book of Ezekiel consists of the direct addresses of the Lord,[1] the form and style in which those words were recorded are attributable to the writer Ezekiel. Ezekiel's style is lofty. He has brought prose and poetry together in one masterpiece. The book abounds with visions, parables, allegories, apocalyptic imagery, and various symbolic acts. Jerome called the book "an ocean and labyrinth of the mysteries of God." Although the interpretations of some of its symbols are difficult, it is a singularly fascinating and interesting book.

Ezekiel apparently had methodical habits of recording events and dates. This is seen especially in connection with the messages he received from God. There are twelve such dated messages in his book.[2] Read each one, and note particularly the year of captivity cited: 1:1-2; 8:1; 20:1; 24:1; 26:1; 29:1; 29:17; 30:20; 31:1; 32:1; 32:17; 40:1. The methodical style of Ezekiel is also seen in the orderly organization of his book, the outline of which we will now begin to study in the survey exercise.

---

1. Scan the book, and note the frequency of the phrase "and the word of the Lord came unto me, saying."
2. There are other datelines besides these dated messages in the book (cf. 33:21).

15

II. SURVEY OF THE BOOK

Survey study is the first big step in the study of the text of a book of the Bible. It is the broad, general study of the large movements, preparatory to an analysis of the parts. It is like the skyscraper view of a city that one sees before making a tour of the streets and buildings below.

For your survey study, use the following suggestions before learning Chart C.

1. Read the entire book, in one sitting if possible. This should be only a cursory reading, for main impressions and observations of atmosphere. It is not an analytical reading. What are your impressions after this reading? Record these.

_____

_____

_____

2. Secure a chapter title for each of Ezekiel's forty-eight chapters, and record them on a chart similar to Chart B.

EZEKIEL 1—48   **Chart B**

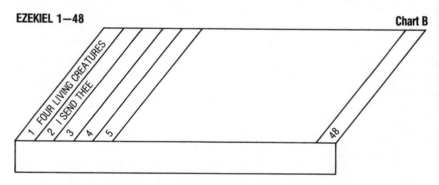

3. Now begin to look for groupings of chapters, according to similar content. Outline your findings on the chart.
4. Is there any turning point in the book? If so, locate it on your chart.
5. Record words and phrases that are repeated throughout the book. Such words and phrases, if they are strong, are clues to the theme of the book.

6. From this introductory study of the text, what does the book teach about God?

_____

_____

About the prophet Ezekiel?

_____

_____

About the people?

_____

_____

Now study the accompanying survey chart (Chart C), checking the outlines with your own personal study.

Observe the following concerning Chart C:

1. Basically the book of Ezekiel is made up of three main parts:

Fate of Judah (desolation)
Foes of Judah (destruction)
Future of Judah and Israel (restoration)

Actually, the first three chapters could be considered a separate introductory division in the book, recording the call and commission of Ezekiel. But since the commission of Ezekiel involved pronouncing the judgment of captivity, these three chapters may rightly be placed in the large division called "Fate of Judah."

2. There is a turning point in the book, made up of two parts. At 24:2 Ezekiel is informed by God that the king of Babylon has begun the siege against Jerusalem. At 33:21, the actual turning point, Ezekiel learns from a messenger that the city has fallen. Up to 24:2, Ezekiel's message is mainly "The city shall be destroyed." After 33:21, Ezekiel looks to the next prophetic peak and prophesies, "The city shall be restored." It is at chapter 24 that the prophet learns that, when Jerusalem falls, his tongue will be loosed to speak a new message of hope; and people, sobered by the reality of Jerusalem's destruction, will begin to give him a hearing. (Read 24:25-27.) The middle section (chaps. 25-32) concerns the foreign nations. At first glance this may appear to be out of place in the outline of the book. Considering the broad context noted above, show how this section is appropriately located here. Is restoration promised any of these Gentile nations?

3. If the book of Ezekiel were divided into two main parts, the division would then be at chapter 33. Note the outline "Jehovah Not There;" "Jehovah There." In the first division God is represented as leaving the city (chaps. 10-11); in the last division He

17

SURVEY CHART OF EZEKIEL

Chart C

EZEKIEL	THE GLORY OF THE LORD

A KEY VERSE: 1:28b

	JUDGMENT TO COME					RESTORATION TO COME	
CALL AND COMMISSION	PREDICTION OF JUDGMENT	REASON FOR JUDGMENT	CERTAINTY OF JUDGMENT	RIGHTEOUSNESS OF JUDGMENT	UNIVERSALITY OF JUDGMENT	ANTICIPATION	REALIZATION
	JERUSALEM'S DESTRUCTION	JERUSALEM'S INIQUITY	SYMBOLS AND SERMONS PREDICTING JERUSALEM'S FALL		JUDGMENTS AGAINST FOREIGN NATIONS	ISRAEL'S RESURRECTION	ISRAEL'S NEW LIFE

1   4   8   12   20   25   33   38   40   44   47   48

33 NATION REGATHERED
38 NATION REESTABLISHED
40 NEW TEMPLE
44 NEW WORSHIP
47 NEW LAND

FATE OF JUDAH —desolation—   FOES OF JUDAH —destruction—   FUTURE OF JUDAH AND ISRAEL —restoration—

Jehovah not there   Jehovah there (48:35)

7 YEARS of prophesying   15 YEARS of prophesying

GLORY DEPARTED (9:3; 10:4, 18, 19; 11:22-23)   GLORY ON EARTH (43:2-6; 44:4)

HEAVENLY GLORY

The siege has begun   TURNING POINT "The city is smitten" (33:21)

THE CITY SHALL BE DESTROYED   THE CITY SHALL BE RESTORED

B.C. 559

586

588

593

is shown as returning (43:1-5) and remaining (48:35). Note how chapters 10 and 11 depict God withdrawing *gradually* and *reluctantly*. In 10:4, He is standing over the threshold of His house. In 10:18 He moves and stands over the cherubim; in 10:19 He is at the door of the east gate. Finally, in 11:22-23, He pauses again upon the Mount of Olives east of Jerusalem, as though bidding a last farewell of the city where He had set His name. One is reminded of the way Christ, hundreds of years later, looked back on the same city whose inhabitants had rejected Him, and cried: "O Jerusalem, Jerusalem, . . . how often would I have gathered thy children together, even as a hen gathereth her chickens under her wings, and ye would not!" (Matt. 23:37).

4. Study the outline, which breaks down the large divisions into smaller sections (Call and Commission; Judgment Foretold; etc.). Compare these groupings with those you observed in your earlier study. Make a note of these sections in your Bible.

A few comments may be made here concerning the last division of the book, RESTORATION TO COME (chaps. 33-48). This division has two distinct sections: the first consists of seven chapters, dealing principally with prophecies anticipating the final restoration of Israel; the second consists of nine chapters, dealing with Israel in the land, especially with reference to the Temple.

Notice especially the Shepherd chapter (chap. 34), and compare it with the Shepherd Psalm (Ps. 23) and the Shepherd chapter in John (chap. 10). Read carefully 36:16-23 and observe that Ezekiel agrees with all the prophets, from Moses downward, that Israel's restoration is not to be because of anything in themselves but for the glory of God's great name, and to convince all mankind of the same thing, that His judgments shall make manifest that "I am the Lord."

The famous vision of the valley of dry bones (chap. 37) is more remarkable in some ways than any which has preceded it. It is the Spirit of the Lord alone who can gather the helpless, dismembered, denationalized people and make them a living body once more. Today's newspapers are recording the initial fulfillments of these prophecies.

The last vision which Ezekiel sees is of the restored Temple (chaps. 40-48). The chief point of this vision is that the glory of the Lord, which Ezekiel had seen departing from the first Temple, is now seen to return and abide in this Temple.

5. Study the other parts of the survey chart (Chart C), until you are thoroughly acquainted with it. In future studies, whenever you analyze a chapter of Ezekiel, refer to this chart first to review the surrounding context of that chapter.

III. KEY PHRASES

You have already observed how certain phrases in Ezekiel are emphasized by repetition. Some of the outstanding ones are listed here:

"Son of man" appears more than ninety times in Ezekiel. The prophet is the one so designated. The title was symbolic of Ezekiel's identity with the people to whom he was sent, even as Jesus the Son of Man was so identified. This title was Jesus' favorite title of Himself (appears almost ninety times in the gospels). Ezekiel has been called "the other Son of Man."

"The word of the Lord came unto me" appears forty-nine times.

"Glory of the God of Israel" or *"glory of the Lord"* appears eleven times in the first eleven chapters.

"Lord God" appears more than two hundred times.

"I shall be sanctified in thee" appears six times. (Read 20:41; 28:22, 25; 36:23; 38:16; 39:27.)

"The hand of the Lord was upon me" appears seven times: 1:3; 3:14, 22; 8:1; 33:22; 37:1; 40:1.

"I have wrought with you for my name's sake" appears five times: 20:44; cf. 36:22; 20:9, 14, 22.

IV. MAIN SUBJECTS

The glory and majesty of the Lord constitute the prominent subject of the book of Ezekiel. A key verse for the book could thus be 1:28*b*. (Consider other key verses, such as 1:1*b*; 3:23; 2:3.) A title suggested is "The Glory of the Lord."

Some of the main subjects of Ezekiel are in the following list. At some time during the course of your study identify various passages that speak about these.

Attributes of God
    His glory
    His sovereignty
    His name
    His holiness
    His justice
    His mercy
Man
    individual responsibility
    corrupt heart

Israel
idolatry[3]
judgment: its causes, certainty, and righteousness
elect nation
hope
Gentile Nations
accountability
judgment
Last Days
restored kingdom

V. VISIONS

Ezekiel is known as "The Prophet of Visions." The very first verse of his book reads "The heavens were opened, and I saw visions of God." A vision in Bible days was a miraculous experience of a man of God on a special occasion, whereby God revealed truth to him in some pictorial and audible form. Visions were of all kinds, differing in such things as length, intensity, number of symbols, and whether the vision was perceived in the spirit (as in a dream) or by the physical senses.

Here are the visions that are recorded in Ezekiel:

1. Vision of the Cherubim (Vision of God):	
Ezekiel's inaugural vision	1:4-28
2. Vision of the Roll	2:9-3:3
3. Vision on the Plain	3:22-23
4. Visions of Jerusalem	
a. four abominations in the Temple	8:1-18
b. inhabitants slain	9:1-11
c. city destroyed by fire	10:1-22
d. the Lord departs from the city	11:1-25
5. Vision of Dry Bones	37:1-10
6. Visions of the New Temple	
and Associated Scenes	40:1–48:35

3. One writer has commented on Israel's apostasy thus: "Israel's proneness to idolatry is depicted by the prophet under the figure of a wife's infidelity. This he does in the long sixteenth chapter, and the almost equally long twenty-third chapters. In these chapters the relentless realism of our author's methods is most startling. The subject is a loathsome one. The instinct of delicacy is to escape from it as speedily as possible. But Ezekiel means not merely to suggest the picture to us, but to make us see it. . . . It is not dreadful to read, but the result is such an expression of the odiousness of apostasy from God as is without parallel in literature" (Ballantine).

VI. OTHER FORMS OF REVELATION TO EZEKIEL

Besides speaking to Ezekiel through visions, God revealed Himself and His ways to the prophet in various other forms. These are listed below. Be sure to read the passages cited, and try to identify the truths which God was teaching Ezekiel and the people of Judah.

A. Symbolic Actions

Ezekiel, perhaps more than any other prophet, taught by symbolic *actions*—those strange things God asked His prophets to do in order that His messages might impress the people vividly and intensely. God told Ezekiel, "I have set thee for a sign unto the house of Israel" (12:6). So his symbolic actions were revelatory signs. Some of the things he was commanded to do must have been extremely hard and trying. He was continually exposing himself to the jeers and scorn of the skeptical. Read the first recorded act of this kind in chapter 4. Someone has written of this, "What curiosity and comment he would excite as he would lie on the street corner in one position for many days, with a brick in front of him on which was drawn the City of Jerusalem, and before which he enacted a miniature battle and siege. How like the act of a fanatic or madman this would appear to the thoughtless!" There were probably similar reactions to the shaving of his hair (chap. 5), the removing of his household goods (chap. 12), and the joining of two sticks (chap. 37). But hardest of all these symbolic prophecies was the death of Ezekiel's wife—his "heart's desire" (24:15-18). Like Aaron, when his two sons were struck dead, Ezekiel was bidden, "Neither shalt thou mourn nor weep, neither shall thy tears run down; forbear to cry, make no mourning for the dead."

But the symbolic acts produced the desired effect, at least upon the hearts of the serious-minded, causing them to ask what these things meant (see 12:9; 24:19; 37:18). This was the prophet's opportunity to explain their significance and drive home the application. "In the work of God no man may turn or falter; no sound of breaking human heart may mar the full majestic music of a prophet's voice, speaking to all ages from the mount of cloud and vision."

Following is a list of the main symbolic actions of Ezekiel:

Sign	Teaching	Passage
1. Sign of the Brick	Jerusalem's siege and fall	4:1-3
2. Sign of the Prophet's Posture	Discomforts of captivity	4:4-8
3. Sign of Famine	Deprivations of captivity	4:9-17
4. Sign of the Knife and Razor	Utter destruction of the city	5:1-17
5. Sign of House Moving	Removal to another land	12:1-7; 17-20
6. Sign of the Sharpened Sword	Judgment imminent	21:1-17
7. Sign of Nebuchadnezzar's Sword	Babylon the captor	21:18-23
8. Sign of the Smelting Furnace	Judgment and purging	22:17-31
9. Sign of Ezekiel's Wife's Death	Blessings forfeited	24:15-27
10. Sign of the Two Sticks	Reunion of Israel and Judah	37:15-17

B. Allegories

Allegories in the Bible are stories intended to teach spiritual lessons. John Bunyan's *The Pilgrim's Progress* is a classic example of an allegory. In Ezekiel the allegories have the same purpose as the symbolic actions. They differ in that the allegories teach by words; the symbolic actions teach by actual events. Below are listed the main allegories of Ezekiel. Read each allegory, and record the spiritual lesson it teaches.

Allegory	Teaching	Passage
1. The Vine		15:1-8
2. The Faithless Wife		16:1-63
3. The Two Eagles[4]		17:1-21
4. The Cedar		17:22-24
5. The Two Women		23:1-49
6. The Boiling Caldron		24:1-14

C. Apocalyptic Imagery

Apocalyptic writing prophesies of things to come by means of much symbol and imagery. Daniel and Revelation are the two books of the Bible usually classified as apocalyptic. Ezekiel contains many apocalyptic passages. Identify the contents of each of the following:

4. This story, along with that of the boiling caldron (24:1-14), may be classified as a parable, as 17:1-2 and 24:3 identify them.

6:1-14
7:5-12
20:33-44
28:25-26
34:25-31
36:8-15, 33-36
38:1-23
39:1-29
47:1-12

There are many resemblances between Ezekiel and Revelation. This is clearly seen when passages like the following are compared:

Ezekiel	Revelation	Ezekiel	Revelation
1:1	19:11	14:21	6:8
1:5	4:6	26:13	18:22
1:10	4:7	27:28-30	18:17-19
1:22	4:6	37:10	11:11
1:24	1:15	37:27	21:3
1:28	4:3	38:2-3	20:8
2:9	5:1	40:2	21:10
3:1, 3	10:10	40:3	11:1
7:2	7:1	43:2	1:15
9:4	7:3	43:16	21:16
9:11	1:13	47:1, 12	22:1-2
10:2	8:5	48:31	21:12

D. Poems

In Ezekiel, the poems are lamentations, or elegies. They are found at 19:1-14 and 27:1-36.

VII. MESSIANIC PASSAGES

The chief messianic passages of Ezekiel, as listed in *The Wycliffe Bible Commentary*, are:
    1. The Lord, the sanctuary   11:16-20
    2. The wonderful cedar sprig   17:22-24
    3. The rightful King   21:26-27

4. The faithful Shepherd	34:11-31
5. The great purification	36:25-35
6. The great resurrection	37:1-14
7. The great reunion	37:21-28
8. The overthrow of Gog	38:1–39:29
9. The life-giving stream	47:1-12

You will want to make a careful study of each of these important passages prophesying of Christ.

VIII. MAJOR SPIRITUAL LESSONS OF EZEKIEL

Most of this lesson has been devoted to a survey and description of the highlights of the book of Ezekiel. As a summary exercise, review this lesson and then write a list of the major spiritual lessons of Ezekiel. Identify first what God was teaching Ezekiel and the exiles; then derive the universal timeless truths that apply to today.

Lesson 3

Ezekiel's Vision Call and Commission

Ezekiel and his fellow exiles, living in houses along the river Chebar, had seen many uneventful days and weeks and months come and go. The hardships and privations had become part of their life. It was on one of those ordinary dark days that God opened the heavens, put His hand on the thirty-year-old priest Ezekiel, and let him see visions that were to make a different man out of him (1:1-3).

Other men of God saw visions of God (theophanies), but Ezekiel's vision is the most detailed one. For comparative study, read the theophanies of Moses (Ex. 24:9-12); Isaiah (Isa. 6); Jeremiah (Jer. 1:4-10); Daniel (Dan. 7:9-14); John (Rev. 4:2-11).

Ezekiel's vision preceded his call to the prophetic ministry. In this lesson we shall analyze the three chapters that record the vision (1:4-28); the call (2:1-2); and the commission (2:3–3:27).

I. ANALYSIS OF 1:4-28

After reading the passage once, record your impression and reactions. The following observations and conclusions are a starter for analysis:

1. The passage abounds in symbols.
2. Some symbols are difficult to visualize.
3. There are groups of symbols (e.g., things said about wings and things said about wheels).
4. Interpretations should not aim at every detail but concentrate on the large parts of the vision.

Before you seek to interpret the vision, organize your observations as to the parts of the vision. These may be recorded in the boxes shown in Chart D. Use one-word observations whenever possible.

26

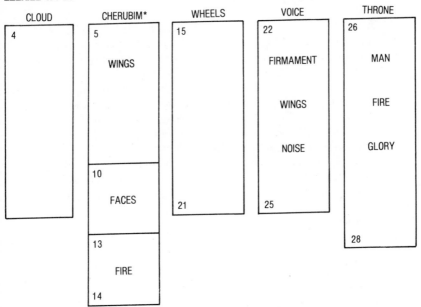

1. Observe that the vision begins in brightness (v. 4) and ends in brightness (v. 28). In what ways is the last paragraph (vv. 26-28) a climax to the vision?

2. Observe this general progression in the vision: still pictures, motion, sound. How does the last phrase, "I heard a voice," introduce the next chapters?

3. List some of the immediate general impressions that you think were Ezekiel's as he saw this vision.

*The four living creatures (1:5) are identified as the cherubim in 10:15, 20. (Cf. 1 Kings 6:23-28; Gen. 3:24; Ps. 18:10.)

A symbol in the Bible may have more than one interpretation. For example, light may speak of dazzling glory or enlightenment on one's path. When the surrounding context of the symbolic word or phrase is nonsymbolic, the symbol is usually easily interpreted by that context. But when the surrounding context is also symbolic, as in this vision of Ezekiel, the interpretative stage is more difficult. Commentaries afford good help in interpreting symbols, but the Bible student should seek such help only after he himself has tried to interpret the symbols.

Most symbols in the Bible relate to everyday life. In the list below, some meanings are already suggested. Add to the list other possible meanings of each symbol, as they appear to you.[1]

Whirlwind—

power, threat

Great cloud—

sign in heaven

Fire—

judgment, purging, brightness

Number 4—

universal (four corners of earth)

Faces—

personality, creature

Wings—

speed, protection, service

Feet—

Hands—

Straight forward—

1. In order to keep the list short, some symbols, such as colors and actions, are not listed. Actually, symbolic actions are sometimes the most important symbols in a vision like this.

Man—
intelligence
_____

Lion—
dignity, supremacy
_____

Ox—
strength, service
_____

Eagle—
speed,
_____

Lamps—

_____

Lightning—

_____

Wheel—

_____

Wheel in . . . a wheel (interpreted by 17b)—

_____

_____

Eyes—
sight
_____

Spirit—
Holy Spirit, activity, guidance
_____

_____

Firmament—

_____

Noise—

_____

Bow (rainbow)

_____

Now read the vision again, and derive the most appropriate interpretation from each symbol. Keep in mind that the entire vision was a vision of *God*.

Next try to answer the following questions:

1. What does the likeness of the cherubim reveal about God?

_____

_____

2. What different things are said about the compound wheel?

_____

_____

What is learned about God from this?

_____

3. Compare "the spirit" of verse 20 with "the spirit" of 2:2. What is taught about the spirit in verse 20?

_____

4. Why do wings play an important part in this vision about God?

_____

_____

_____

5. What attributes of God are symbolized in the paragraph about the throne (vv. 26-28)?

_____

6. Go back over the entire vision, and list the symbols that speak of God's

omnipresence: _____

sovereignty: _____

majesty: _____

omniscience: _____

activity: _____

omnipotence: _____

holiness: _____

mercy: _____

1. The cherubim, or four living creatures, of this vision have suggested various truths to Bible students. One interpretation is this: "Man is exalted among creatures; the eagle is exalted among birds; the ox is exalted among domestic animals; the lion is exalted among the wild beasts; and all of them have received dominion, and greatness has been given them, yet they are stationed below the chariot of the Holy One."[2] Each of the four gospels is likened to each of the creatures, according to the picture of Christ it emphasizes: Matthew, the lion (Matthew presents Christ as King of the Jews; cf. "the Lion of the tribe of Judah," Rev. 5:5); Mark, the ox (Mark presents Christ as the Servant); Luke, the man (Luke presents Christ as the Son of Man); John, the eagle (John presents Christ as the Son of God).

2. The compound wheel ("wheel in the middle of a wheel," v. 16) probably was so constructed that one wheel was inside the rim of the other and at right angels to it. The intended suggestion is that it always *moves forward*, without turning (cf. 17*b*). The entire picture is that of a unique chariot moving over the face of the earth.

II. ANALYSIS OF 2:1–3:27

A. Ezekiel's Call (2:1-2)

The call of God to a man for service is usually brief, for basically only one response is the issue, namely, submission. What is taught about divine call by the following:
1. "Stand"

_____

2. "The spirit entered into me"

_____

3. "The spirit . . . set me upon my feet"

_____

4. "I heard him"

_____

2. A rabbinical interpretation, quoted in Charles F. Pfeiffer and Everett F. Harrison, eds., *The Wycliffe Bible Commentary* (Chicago: Moody, 1962), p. 710.

B. Ezekiel's Commission (2:3–3:27)

Many spiritual lessons may be learned from this passage. Before you read it, mark off the paragraph divisions in your Bible as they appear on Chart E.

EZEKIEL 2:3—3:27   **Chart E**

Key words: "I send thee"	SWEET	STRONG	GLORY	WATCHMAN	"Arise, go"
2:3	2:8	3:4	3:12	3:16	3:22 / 3:27
COMMISSION	PROPHET'S MESSAGE	PROPHET'S RECEPTION	PROPHET'S VISIONS	PROPHET'S RESPONSIBILITY	COMMISSION AMPLIFIED

Now read the passage, underlining key phrases in your Bible as you read. Record these in the blank spaces of Chart E. Let these phrases be the objects of your main analysis. Note emphases, contrasts, repetitions, relations. After you have carefully worked this out, you will have a good understanding of the prophet's commission. In the course of your analysis, study the outlines shown on Chart E.

The following study questions will suggest other lines of inquiry in this passage.

1. What does 2:5b suggest as to how people should respond to fulfilled prophecy?

_____

_____

2. Was the success of Ezekiel's mission dependent on the people's responding favorably to his preaching?

_____

3. Compare the two uses of the word "rebellious" in 2:8.

_____

_____

4. What is symbolized by the command "Fill thy bowels with this roll" (3:3)?

Account for the sweetness of the scroll's taste (3:3), in view of the bitter message written on it (2:10).

_____

_____

5. What was the significance of each experience of Ezekiel in 3:12-15?

_____

_____

_____

_____

_____

6. Observe the command of 3:22 and the obedient response of 3:23. When was Ezekiel to refrain from speaking?

_____

_____

7. Read the entire passage again and note each place where God ministered or promised to minister to Ezekiel.
8. Write a list of the main spiritual lessons taught by this story of Ezekiel's commission.

Notes

1. The phrase "the spirit" in this and other similar passages of Ezekiel refers to the Holy Spirit.
2. The name "Lord God" in Ezekiel translates the Hebrew *Adonai Yahweh*. *Adonai* is translated individually as "Lord," and *Yahweh* is translated as "Lord," but when they appear together they are translated in our English Bibles as "Lord God." As indicated in an earlier lesson, this name appears more than two hundred times in Ezekiel.

3. Ezekiel's eating of the scroll containing words from God was one of the prophet's symbolic actions intended to teach an important truth. The scroll (animal skin) became sweet to his taste, symbolizing the sweetness of obedience to God even though tragedy and judgment were involved.

4. On the subject of Ezekiel the watchman, or sentinel, read chapters 18 and 33 for a fuller treatment.

III. SUMMARY

For a summary exercise, be able to tell the story of Ezekiel's call and commission, using the following set of seven commands:

1. "Stand upon thy feet"		2:1
2. "Be not afraid"		2:6
3. "Hear what I say"		2:8
4. "Eat this roll"		3:1
5. "Go speak"		3:1
6. "Give them warning"		3:17
7. "Arise, go forth"		3:22

Lesson 4

Ezekiel's New Audience

The turning point in Ezekiel is at 33:21, when news of Jerusalem's destruction reached the prophet. Up until then, Ezekiel was telling his fellow exiles not to expect freedom to return to Jerusalem, because Jerusalem was destined to fall by the judgment of God. On occasion the prophet spoke of a future restoration, but primarily his message was one of judgment.

But now the day of judgment had arrived, and Jerusalem had fallen. So God commissioned Ezekiel to a *new* ministry, one of restoration. His audience of citizens without a city comprised two groups: the newly deported survivors of the siege against Jerusalem who had lived in the city until its destruction, and the exiles of the earlier deportations. Both groups had persistently refused to believe that Jerusalem would fall (cf. 11:1-3).

This was Ezekiel's *new audience*, and the beginning of his ministry to them is described for us in chapter 33.

As preparation for your analysis of chapter 33, review Chart C, recalling the context of this chapter. Also, read chapters 33-39 in their entirety, to sense the anticipatory tone of this section. We saw in the survey study (Chart C) that chapters 40-48 describe the new Temple, and the new Jerusalem and the new land. Chapters 33-39 anticipate that final restoration, as indicated in the outline in Chart F.[1]

I. ANALYSIS OF 33:1-33

First read through the entire chapter for initial observations and impressions.

1. Outline by John Phillips, *Exploring the Scriptures* (Chicago: Moody, 1965), p. 161.

ANTICIPATING FINAL RESTORATION ——▶		THE NEW JERUSALEM	
33	TROUBLES REMOVED	37	TRIBES REGATHERED	40	TEMPLE REBUILT	48	TITLE RESTORED

Verse 21 divides this chapter into two parts. See Chart G. Read chapter 18, and note how similar it is to 33:1-20. In other words, the first half of chapter 33 is a summary of the message that Ezekiel had been preaching *prior* to Jerusalem's fall. His message during those seven years (see Chart C) was mainly minatory (warnings of judgment). Beginning on the day[2] the messenger arrived with the news of Jerusalem's fall, Ezekiel's message was mainly consolatory, prophesying of ultimate restoration in the millennial kingdom.

Refer to Chart G again, and note how chapter 33 is related to chapter 24. Read the passages cited on the diagram. Note the exact fulfillment of prophecy concerning the messenger. Note also that Ezekiel's oracles were directed to the foreign nations during the time of the siege.

With this orientation, begin now to analyze chapter 33 paragraph by paragraph. Record your observations. Use the following study procedures.

1. Read 33:1-9. What various truths about responsibility are taught here?

_____

_____

_____

2. Read 33:10-11. Study these strong words in their context: sins, live, death, turn, why, no pleasure. What is taught about God here?

_____

_____

3. Read 33:12-16. What conditions for living and dying are cited here?

_____

_____

_____

2. The messenger arrived six months after the fall. See Charles F. Pfeiffer and Everett F. Harrison, eds., *The Wycliffe Bible Commentary* (Chicago: Moody, 1962), p. 751, for an explanation of the date problem of verse 21.

ANALYSIS OF EZEKIEL 33:1-33

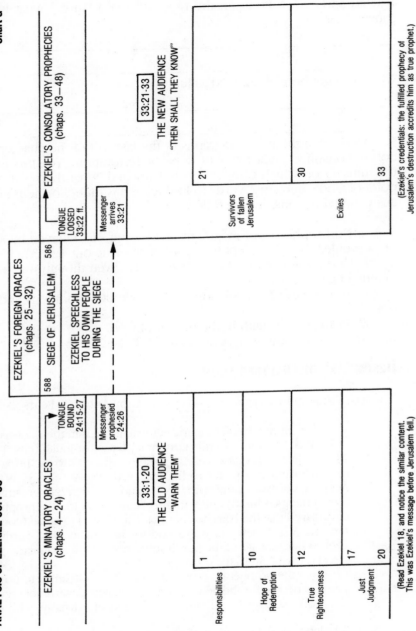

EZEKIEL'S MINATORY ORACLES (chaps. 4—24)

EZEKIEL'S FOREIGN ORACLES (chaps. 25—32)

EZEKIEL'S CONSOLATORY PROPHECIES (chaps. 33—48)

TONGUE BOUND 24:15-27

588   SIEGE OF JERUSALEM   586

TONGUE LOOSED 33:22 ff.

EZEKIEL SPEECHLESS TO HIS OWN PEOPLE DURING THE SIEGE

Messenger prophesied 24:26

Messenger arrives 33:21

33:1-20

THE OLD AUDIENCE "WARN THEM"

33:21-33

THE NEW AUDIENCE "THEN SHALL THEY KNOW"

1

Responsibilities

10

Hope of Redemption

12

True Righteousness

17

Just Judgment

20

21

Survivors of fallen Jerusalem

30

Exiles

33

(Read Ezekiel 18, and notice the similar content. This was Ezekiel's message before Jerusalem fell.)

(Ezekiel's credentials: the fulfilled prophecy of Jerusalem's destruction accredits him as true prophet.)

4. Read 33:17-20. Note again the repeated word "turn." What is conversion?

_____

_____

What is taught here about God as Judge?

_____

_____

5. Observe that the two paragraphs of the last half of the chapter do not contain explicit notes of hope or restoration.[3] Yet, this is the ministry on which Ezekiel is now launched. What then is the point of God's minatory words to Ezekiel at this time? For help in answering this, consider the following:

    a. No prophecy—of judgment *or* blessing—is believed by a person unless he will accept the prophet as a true one (v. 33).
    b. God's word of prophecy is *one* word, even though it is of judgment and blessing.
    c. Prophecies of consolation are not without conditions and demands.
    d. Saving faith is faith in the *person* of God.
6. Compare the endings of paragraphs 21-29 and 30-33.

II. SUMMARY OF CHAPTERS 33-39

The following summary of these chapters is by Anton T. Pearson:

> The fall of Jerusalem marks a turning point in the ministry of Ezekiel. The hitherto minatory oracles against Judah (chs. 1-24) and her pagan foes (chs. 25-32) now give way to the hortatory messages of a pastor to his shattered people (chs. 33-39). After the collapse of the state (33:21) and the complete prostration of people's minds under their calamities (33:10), the prophet declared that the Lord had not made a full end to Israel (contrast ch. 35). A new era was ahead for her. In moving words, Ezekiel here speaks of the purification, restoration and peace of Israel (chs. 34; 36:16 ff.; 37).
>
> First the prophet is recommissioned as a watchman to prepare his people for the new age (ch. 33). A new government under God's servant David will supplant the old dynasty, whose

---

3. Some have interpreted the word "this" of verse 33 to refer to future redemption. But the parallel passage in chapter 24 (see the context of 24:24) hardly allows this interpretation. The first messages of consolation appear in the next chapter (e.g., 34:11 ff.).

wicked shepherds (rulers) scattered the sheep (ch. 34). Israel's territorial integrity will be assured by the desolation of Mount Seir and other enemies (ch. 35), while Israel will experience both outward restoration (36:1-15) and inward restoration (36:16-38). The reintegration of the people into one nation under one King, David, is symbolized by the resurrection of the dry bones and the joining of the two sticks (ch. 37). The peace of restored Israel will be perpetual, for the Lord will protect her miraculously from the threatened invasion of Gog in the latter days (chs. 38; 39).[4]

4. Pfeiffer and Harrison, p. 750.

Lesson 5

The Resurrection of Israel

Prophecies of Israel's resurrection, revealed to Ezekiel more than 2,500 years ago, have begun to be fulfilled recently. Thus far there have been three stages in Israel's national resurrection in the last few decades:

1. Return of the Jews to the Holy Land (on a large scale since World War II)

2. Inauguration of the new state of Israel (May 14, 1948)

3. Successful military campaigns against Arab countries (1956, 1967)

Current history is clearly telling the people and nations of the world that Israel does have a place in God's timetable of future events and that God has not cast off Israel forever. Because the deed of the land of Palestine will revert once more to Israel by divine direction, the world will one day have to recognize that God, the Creator of the universe, after all does own the land.

Ezekiel's prophecies in chapters 33-48 follow a general chronological progression, shown in Chart H.

PROGRESSION OF PROPHECIES   Chart H

chap. 33	chaps. 37—39	chaps. 40—48
Jerusalem destroyed, and Israel in exile*	Israel regathered and established	Israel worshiping God in the millennial kingdom
586 B.C.	Today	Near Future

*This exile terminated after seventy years, when the Jews returned to Jerusalem, but the restoration was only temporary. Worldwide dispersion was the lot of the Jews thereafter.

Before there can be a millennial kingdom (chaps. 40-48), the Jews must be regathered to the land (even though in unbelief) and converted in heart to accept Jesus Christ as their King David (chaps. 37–39). The regathering is now in progress; the conversion is yet to come.

I. ANALYSIS

The analytical studies of this lesson are of three parts, following the general outline of Ezekiel 37-48, which is as follows:

A. Israel's regathering to the land (chap. 37)
B. Israel's victories over attacking foes (chaps. 38-39)
C. Israel's life in the millennial age (chaps. 40-48)

Because of the length of this portion of Ezekiel, it is suggested that you divide the lesson into three study units, following the threefold outline shown. Study at one time only what you can do thoroughly.

A. Israel's Regathering to the Land (37:1-28)

This prophecy was revealed by a vision and by a symbolic action. Read the chapter, observing this organization:

1. vision of dry bones (37:1-11)
2. interpretation (37:11-14)
3. symbol of the two sticks (37:15-18)
4. interpretation (37:19-20)
5. amplified interpretation of the vision and the symbol (37:21-28)

Reread the chapter, observing how clearly it is shown that God is the One who acts in the story. Note such phrases as "I will make," "I will take," "I will be," "I will open." Observe that miracles abound in the action. This is important for you to recognize; otherwise your tendency might be to discount any *literal* interpretation of the seemingly impossible events that appear in these last prophecies of Ezekiel. (An illustration of such a spirit of rejection of the miraculous element is the liberal critics' denial of the historicity of many of the fantastic events in the Israelites' wilderness journeys recorded in Numbers.)

For your next exercise, make a list of the various events in the experience of Israel that are prophesied in the chapter. At this point you need not try to determine when or how these events would transpire. Compare your list with the following:

Recompense	(v. 11)
Revival	(v. 12a)

41

Regathering	(v. 12*b*)
Recognition	(vv. 13-14)
Reunion	(vv. 15-22)
Repentance	(v. 23)
Regeneration	(vv. 23*b* ff.)

After you have carefully studied the symbols as they have been interpreted by the text itself, proceed to the next step of your study, *application*, which relates the fulfillment of the prophecies to world history. That is, when and how will these things happen? There are various schools of thought about this. Three of the views are:

1. Return of the Jews to Jerusalem after the Babylonian exile (535 B.C.). Literal application.

2. Ecumenism's one united world church, as God's "people" (twentieth century). Figurative application.

3. Return of the Jews to Palestine from worldwide dispersion (twentieth century). Literal application.

In answering the question given above, it will help you to know what the New Testament says about Israel's future. For clear New Testament teaching that Israel would play a vital part in history subsequent to New Testament days, read Paul's interpretation in Romans 11. As of Paul's day, God had not cast away His people (Rom. 11:1); the day of Israel's salvation was still future (Rom. 11:26-27). Now, after almost two thousand years of the Church Age, when the gospel of reconciliation has been preached to the Gentile world, the day of Israel's resurrection is dawning (Rom. 11:26). It must be clear to the keen and observing Bible student that the prophecy of Ezekiel 37 is being literally fulfilled today in Israel's resurrection. There has not been repentance nor regeneration yet (Ezek. 37:23-28), but that day will also come, ushering in what is called the millennial (thousand-year) kingdom. Read Revelation 20:1-6 for a brief description of that kingdom.

B. Israel's Victories over Attacking Foes (38:1-39:29)

At some future time,[1] after Israel has settled down in Palestine in

---

1. Rev. 19:11-20:10 gives this general sequence of last days: Battle of Armageddon (19:11-21); Millennium (20:1-6); Battle of Gog and Magog (20:7-10). The Battle of Gog in Ezekiel 38-39 is not the battle of the same name in Rev. 20:7-10. Merrill F. Unger holds that the battle in Ezekiel is subsequent to Armageddon (*Unger's Bible Handbook* [Chicago: Moody, 1966], p. 378); John F. Walvoord says, "The Ezekiel passage seems to refer to an earlier battle, when the army from the North invaded Israel, whereas in this battle [Rev. 19:17-19] God is contending with the armies of the entire world," *The Revelation of Jesus Christ* (Chicago: Moody, 1966), p. 279.

rest and safety (38:8, 11), a coalition of armies led by Gog will attack the land, only to be utterly destroyed by God. This is the story of chapters 38 and 39.

Before analyzing the text of these chapters, it would help you to become acquainted with the geographical names. Refer to a Bible dictionary or commentary for full descriptions. The following brief identifications of the lesser known places summarize the important aspects:

1. *Gog.* This is the name, whether symbolic or literal, of the leader of the coalition of northern powers antagonistic to God and the nation of Israel. The phrase "God and Magog" in Revelation 20:8 has a wider connotation, referring to ungodly nations of the entire world.

2. *Magog.* This is the land of Gog, somewhere north of Palestine. Early Greek writers identified this as the land of the Scythians. "Modern Christian writers indicate the Tartars of Russia and of southern Europe."[2]

3. *Meshech and Tubal.* Peoples living in the region of the Black Sea.

4. *Gomer.* The Cimmerians, who originally lived north of the Black Sea, later settling down in Asia Minor.

5. *Togarmah.* Northeast of Asia Minor, in the region of Armenia ("the uttermost parts of the north," 38:6, RSV*).

6. *Sheba and Dedan.* Great trading centers in Arabia. These names, together with the reference "merchants of Tarshsish," refer to countries engaged in worldwide trade.

Now read the chapters with the view to identifying the main point of each paragraph. Note also key phrases, such as "the heathen shall know that I am the Lord." Record this study in Chart I.

Questions

1. In what *general* geographical region are the nations of 38:1-4, 6 located?

_____

_____

These are joined by nations from what regions (38:5)?

_____

_____

Revised Standard Version.
2. Merrill C. Tenney, ed., *Zondervan Pictorial Bible Dictionary* (Grand Rapids: Zondervan, 1963), p. 502.

PARAGRAPH	MAIN POINT	KEY PHRASES	GOD'S PURPOSES
38:1-9			
10-13			
14-16			
17:23			
CHAPTER 39 is an amplification of the paragraph 38:17-23			
39:1-10	FIRE		
11-16	GRAVES		
17:24	FLESH		
CONCLUSION			
39:25-29			

What part is played by the ones designated in 38:13?

_____

_____

2. Does the attack by Gog and his hosts come before or after Israel has begun to enjoy settling down in the new land?

_____

3. What are God's ultimate purposes in bringing such trials to His chosen people?

_____

_____

4. What is the basic motivation for all offensive wars (cf. 38:12)?

_____

_____

5. Why does the Bible describe such gruesome details of destruction as in these chapters?

_____

_____

6. What does 39:25-29 teach about Israel's experiences and God's ways? Study this paragraph carefully.

_____

_____

7. Write a list of important truths taught by these two chapters, in areas such as:
  The God of History
  The Grace of God
  The Covenant People
  Latter Days

Notes

Details of Israel's future are not all known or clear. Dates, durations, events, people, nations, and places have not been spelled out in biblical prophecy. But the overall pattern has been revealed, and the Bible student thrills to watch God's purposes being fulfilled. For the first time since its destruction in A.D. 70, the old city of Jerusalem, with its site of the original Temple, has been occupied by the Jewish state. This occupation has been strongly challenged, not only by Israel's bordering Arab neighbors but by Russia, the powerful country to the north, and other world powers. Obviously, much history remains to be written concerning Palestine and the holy city of Jerusalem. The stage is being set for the coming kingdom!

C. Israel's Life in the Millennial Age (40:1–48:35)

Before reading this passage and the key New Testament Millennium passage (Rev. 20:1-10), try to see the *large* picture of God's family throughout time and into eternity. This is illustrated by the simple diagram in Chart J.

PICTURE OF GOD'S FAMILY   **Chart J**

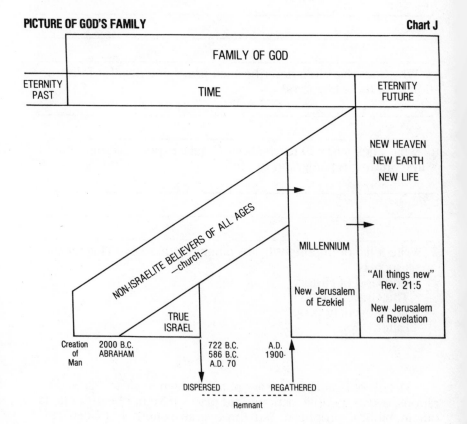

Observe the following on Chart J.

1. Time begins with the creation of the universe, including man; eternity future begins with the new heaven and the new earth.

2. There have been believers in all the ages since man's creation: some are of the house of Israel, indicated here as TRUE IS-RAEL; all others are designated as Gentile believers. (All believers, of whatever times, are saved "by grace ... through faith," Eph. 2:8; cf. Heb. 11.)

3. The Millennium is an earthly kingdom for all believers, Jewish and Gentile.[3] However, because the many kingdom promises given specially to Israel find their fulfillment in the millennial kingdom, this period is particularly Jewish-oriented. The new Jerusalem of Ezekiel is of this period.

4. When all things are made new, after the Millennium, the family of God will be as homogeneous as it ever can be, even as to place of dwelling and experience.

Now read Revelation 20:1-10, followed by Ezekiel 40:1–48:35. The Ezekiel reading may be a tedious exercise, especially in the first half, because of all the dimensions and details. Do not let this bog you down in your study.

Write out a list of your impressions and questions about the descriptions in both passages. Before referring to a commentary for help, consider the following observations, some of which may have been yours also:

1. *Observation:* There is much detail in the Ezekiel account. *Question:* Why? *Possible answers:* (1) If the specifications of the Temple are to be literally followed out in a future construction, the reason for detail is obvious. (2) There is a symbolic intent here: the need for meticulous attention to things dear to the heart of God; also, many spiritual truths may be derived from the various symbols, such as are intended by the symbols of the book of Leviticus.

2. *Observation:* All of the items of the Ezekiel account are those of Israel's life. *Question:* Why is there no reference to Israel in John's account of the Millennium? (Rev. 20:1-10). *Possible answer:* Ezekiel's ministry was to Israel, and his consolatory message concerned *Israel's* millennial hope. John's vision concerned all people, hence no emphasis on one group.

---

3. See Gleason L. Archer, *A Survey of Old Testament Introduction* (Chicago: Moody, 1964), pp. 363-64. Writes Archer, "There are many indications in the Old Testament prophets that Jewish and Gentile believers shall be incorporated into one body politic in the coming age."

3. *Observation:* There are references to sacrifices here, even blood sacrifices. *Question:* Did not Christ's sacrifice of Himself remove the need for animal sacrifice (cf. Heb. 10:12)? *Possible answer:* Even as the observance of the Lord's Supper today commemorates Jesus' death, in the millennial age there will be similar commemorative ceremonies looking to the past. If *thanksgiving* for atonement remains throughout eternity (cf. Rev. 5:11-14), it is appropriate for *commemoration* of the atonement fact to remain.

4. *Observation:* Much space is devoted to these temporal, mundane objects. *Question:* Why are there not likewise long passages in the Bible describing heaven? (E.g., Rev. 21:1–22:5 is the extent of John's description.) *Possible answer:* The Millennium in many ways describes, by its symbols, what heaven will be like. Heaven, after all, can only be described in the human language of symbols recognized in daily life. It is suggested that in one of your studies of Ezekiel 40-48 you look for various symbols that describe the glories of heaven.

In studying the outline of Ezekiel 40-48, you will probably seek the help of a commentary. *The Wycliffe Bible Commentary* has a detailed outline, the three main parts of which are:

A New Temple (40:1–43:27)
A New Service of Worship (44:1–46:24)
A New Holy Land (47:1–48:35)

In your study of the Ezekiel passage, notice the emphasis on the *new*. Compare this with how Revelation ends, noting its references to "new heaven and a new earth" (21:1); "new Jerusalem" (21:2); "all things new" (21:5).

The following questions relate to other important aspects of Ezekiel's text:

1. The holy place and most holy place are described in the chapter showing the arrangement of the Temple (chap. 41). Account for the absence of any reference to the Ark, mercy seat, high priest, or tables of the law.

_____

_____

_____

2. How is God's holiness emphasized in 42:1-20?

_____

_____

Observe references to "separate" and "separation" (e.g., v. 20).

3. Study 43:1-12 for its emphasis on the return of God's glory, its filling of the Temple, and the place of God's throne.

4. What spiritual truths are taught by the picture of the waters issuing from the Temple (47:1-12)?

_____

_____

5. Concerning the boundaries of the land (47:13-23), recall God's promises originally given to Abraham (Gen. 15:18-21) and confirmed to Joshua (Joshua 13:1–19:51). How will the millennial kingdom bring the fulfillment of that promise?

_____

_____

6. What is the last phrase of Ezekiel?

_____

As a summary exercise, relate this phrase to the various parts of the book of Ezekiel, as you have studied them in this manual. Review Chart C to help you in this exercise.

D. Summary of the Book of Ezekiel

At the commencement of his prophetic ministry, Ezekiel was given a vision of the glorious Lord reigning in heaven. The people of israel had once known the blessing of such a glory shining in their midst, but now the glory had departed because of Israel's sin. It was Ezekiel's task to announce to his fellow exiles the coming judgment of desolation of the holy city and captivity of its inhabitants. When the city fell in 586 B.C. God loosed the prophet's tongue to speak the new message of restoration to come, for those who would turn to the Lord. For fifteen years it was his happy privilege to quote the Lord as saying.

> Now will I bring again the captivity of Jacob,
> and have mercy upon the whole house of Israel. . . .
> Then shall they know that I am the LORD their God. . . .
> I have gathered them unto their own land. . . .
> Neither will I hide my face any more from them:
> for I have poured out my spirit upon the house of Israel.
> (39:25, 28-29)

This bright message did not contradict Ezekiel's earlier minatory oracles. The seventy-year captivity must first be fulfilled, and then there would be a return to the land on the part of a believing remnant of a new generation. The Temple would be rebuilt, and the glory of the Lord would come down to Israel again. But Ezekiel's prophecy, like most of the Old Testament consolatory prophecies, referred mainly to a latter-day messianic fulfillment, when Israel would be reestablished in the millennial kingdom and Christ would sit on David's throne. All the bright promises given to the nation could be fulfilled only in Christ, Israel's Messiah.

Such was the ministry of Ezekiel—priest, prophet, and pastor. There is no biographical note in his book as to how his message was received, or what were his experiences for the remainder of his life. Rather, the book closes with the spotlight on the *message*, not the *man*. Thus we who read the book today are exhorted to lift up our eyes and look in the direction of that prophetic message's fulfillment. To read a newspaper headline "Israel Takes the Old City of Jerusalem" makes the Christian rejoice that "the coming of the Lord draweth nigh" (James 5:8). The words of Ezekiel's book are the true words of God, and we who are living today are seeing the beginnings of its glorious fulfillment.

Lesson 6
Background of Daniel

The book of Daniel has been called "the greatest book in the Bible on godless kingdoms and the kingdom of God."[1] The godless kingdoms referred to here are the Gentile nations, and the kingdom of God is the millennial reign centered on Israel. Daniel is a relatively short book, but compacted into its pages are multitudes of fascinating prophecies and basic doctrines that challenge the Bible student to tarry long in its study.

In this lesson we shall devote our attention to the background of the book of Daniel, which includes such subjects as the historical setting of its writing, the man who wrote it, and introductory aspects of the book itself. Though this lesson is not a study of the text of Daniel, you will find that the lesson will be more meaningful if you have first made at least a casual reading of the book.

I. HISTORICAL SETTING

Daniel lived and prophesied at the beginning of a notable epoch in the world's history, referred to by Jesus as "the times of the Gentiles" (cf. Luke 21:24). Concerning this epoch, note these two things:

1. Its distinctive character: During this time, by divine design Gentiles, not Jews, have political power and supremacy in the world.

2. Its duration: The "times of the Gentiles" began with the Babylonian captivity of Judah under Nebuchadnezzar, and it will end with the second coming of Christ in glory (Luke 21:24-27).

---

1. W. Graham Scroggie, *Know Your Bible* (London: Pickering & Inglis, 1940), 1: 199.

God had offered world supremacy to the Jews (Deut. 28) on the condition of obedience to Him, but the Jews would not comply with that condition. So, beginning in 605 B.C. God withdrew the offer and gave the supremacy to the Gentiles, at that time represented by the nation of Babylon. Nebuchadnezzar, king of Babylon, was the first Gentile world ruler to subdue the people of Israel after their establishment in the land of Palestine. Other kings had brought them under tribute for brief periods, but Nebuchadnezzar overturned David's throne, carried away the people, and made the land an integral part of his domain. Nebuchadnezzar, as absolute monarch of Babylon, was thus made master of the world and was offered the opportunity of continuing in power on the same condition of obedience to God.

We shall see in the book before us now that Nebuchadnezzar accepted this gift of power from God. We shall find that it was received in the spirit of self-complacency and pride and used for purposes of self-aggrandizement, not for the glorification of the One who gave it. There has never been a Gentile world power that, as a nation, had had for its *chief* aim the glory of God.

As one contemplates the Jewish captives in Babylon and God's dealings with them there, it would seem that one great object He had in sending Judah into Babylonian exile was to cure the people of idolatry, which had wrought their national ruin. The Jews were now in a land that had ever been noted for the multitude of its idols, just as their forefathers had been in a land of idols in Egypt. In Egypt Jehovah had proved, by a series of supernatural displays, the superiority of the God of the Hebrews over the idols worshiped there. He had demonstrated His wisdom and also His love; but He had especially demonstrated His *power*, as that would more strongly appeal to the darkened heathen mind. So here, in Babylon, by a repeated display of supernatural wisdom, and especially power, God showed forth His superiority over the Babylonian idols in order that His people, as well as these Gentiles, might see the contrast and choose once for all to serve the true God.

God did more than demonstrate His power before the eyes of the subjects and rulers of Babylon. He sent Daniel to the courts of the Babylonish monarchs to represent Him there and to teach the Gentile kings His sovereign will concerning *all* nations of the world. For Gentile, as well as Jew, must learn that continuance of power and blessing is dependent upon rendering worship and obedience to God.

So Daniel was prophet to both Gentile and Jew. He prophesied to the Gentiles concerning the events that would take place among the Gentile nations during the times of the Gentiles, or the time during which political dominion of the earth would be vested in Gentile nations. His mission to Israel mainly concerned the unborn generations of Jews. He prophesied of an eventual messianic kingdom, which God would set up when the time of the Gentiles had been fulfilled (see Chart K).

PROPHECY OF MESSIANIC KINGDOM   **Chart K**

This message of Israel's restoration was essentially the same as that preached by Ezekiel. The difference was that Daniel prophesied much about the Gentile epoch and delivered his messages to a Gentile audience as well as to a Hebrew audience.

Study carefully Chart L.

Observe the following concerning Chart L:

1. Daniel's ministry in Babylon lasted for at least seventy years (605-536 B.C.; Dan. 1:1-6), and he lived in Babylon throughout the entire seventy-year captivity period (536 B.C. is the date referred to in 10:1).

2. Babylon, the land of Jewish exile, served under three powers during Daniel's career: Neo-Babylonian, Median, and Persian. The rulers who play an important part in the book of Daniel are:

Nebuchadnezzar; Belshazzar   (Neo-Babylonian)
Darius the Mede[2]   (Median)
Cyrus   (Persian)

3. In 539 B.C., when Belshazzar was co-regent with Nabonidus, Babylon fell to the Persian King Cyrus. This began the Persian period of supremacy.

4. The return of Jewish exiles to Jerusalem and the beginning of construction on the new Temple began at the end of Daniel's career.

---

2. This Darius has been identified as Gubaru, general under Cyrus, king of Persia, whom Cyrus made governor, or sub-king, over the region of Chaldea (Babylonia). (Cf. 5:31; 6:1; 9:1.)

53

DANIEL AND HIS CONTEMPORARIES

Chart L

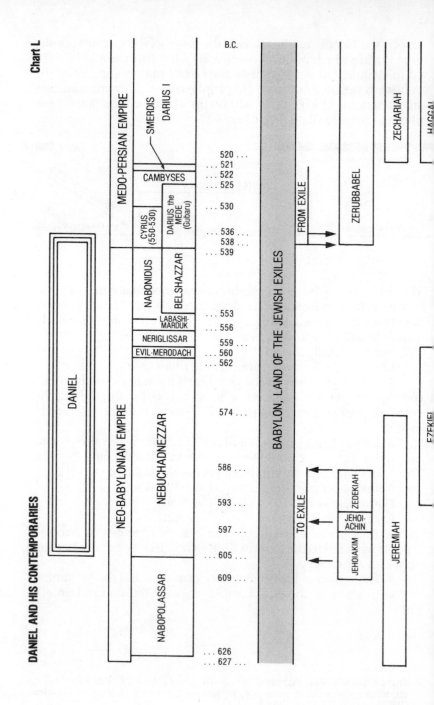

II. THE MAN DANIEL

A. Name

The name Daniel translates the Hebrew word *Daniyye'l*, meaning "God is Judge [Prince]" or "God is my Judge [Prince]." The name given Daniel by Nebuchadnezzar's officer (1:7) was Belteshazzar, meaning "Bel's prince." It was a name honoring one of the pagan gods of Babylon (cf. 4:8; also Isa. 46:1; Jer. 50:2; 51:44).

B. Character

Daniel is usually remembered for his courage and faith, displayed in the experience in the lions' den. He had many other wonderful traits as well. He is one of the few men of whom God writes only good, and he seems to have had in the divine heart in Old Testament days a place such as did John in the New, for three times he is called the "greatly beloved" one (9:23; 10:11, 19). These are some of the outstanding traits of Daniel:

1. *Strong of purpose.* The first striking characteristic noticeable in Daniel is that he was a man of strong purpose. In his heart he resolved that he would not defile himself, that he would live the life of separation from all that God had pronounced unclean. All God's children are called to this life of separation, but how few stand the test! This noble heart-purpose is the key to Daniel's whole life. From first to last he showed this firm, unwavering persistence in whatever he had made up his mind was right for him to do.

2. *Wise, tactful, courteous.* Daniel was also wise, tactful, and courteous. He "requested" of the prince of the eunuchs that he might not defile himself and proposed the ten days' trial of another plan (1:8, 11-13).

3. *Lovable.* Daniel must have been of an exceptionally lovable disposition, for not only God but the prince of the eunuchs loved him tenderly (1:9).

4. *Intelligent and spiritual.* He was, moreover, wonderfully gifted—intellectually and spiritually (1:17, 20); and he was a thorough student of God's written Word, as seen in his familiarity with the books of Moses (9:11-13).

5. *Brave.* Daniel was not lacking in true bravery. He was brave in the solitary hour, as he made resolutions as yet unknown to his adversaries, well aware of the inevitable consequences. He was brave in the public confrontation, and he stood tall and relentless before king and commoner. And he was brave in the critical hour

of judgment by man, very conscious of the unfailing presence of His Lord and God (cf. 3:25).

Daniel stood like a granite mountain. Nothing moved him. He faced the fierce, hungry lions with the same cool, calm faith in God with which he had faced the angry presidents and princes.

6. *Modest and humble.* Daniel's modesty and humility should not be overlooked. He took no credit to himself for having received the interpretation of the dream but gave all honor to God (2:28-30).

7. *Man of faith and prayer.* Chief among Daniel's virtues were his faith in God and his wonderful prayer life. See how his faith is manifested in 2:13-28. Regarding Daniel's prayer life, read 6:10, and observe that his praying was in faith, it was reverent, it was daily, and it was habitual. That is the reason why, in times of peril, it was potent. One should not presume that prayer is just for emergency situations. The deliverance of Daniel came as the result of a *life* of prayer.

C. Biography

Daniel was born into a Judean family of nobility, around the time of the reformation under King Josiah (621 B.C.). Some identify Daniel as one of King Hezekiah's descendants, prophesied in 2 Kings 20:17-18 and Isaiah 39:7 (cf. Dan. 1:3). He was in his late teens when he was taken captive in the first deportation of 605 B.C. In the same group were three other young men no less noble than himself in character. These four youths were handsome, intelligent, and well educated (1:4), and it is not to be wondered at that King Nebuchadnezzar selected them to be trained for his service. He changed their residence, their names, their occupation, their language, their food, but he could not change their character. That, he had to find, would shine forth in spite of everything. They were given names derived from the names of the gods of Babylon; but they had no intention of worshiping those gods, nor of doing as the Babylonians did, just because now they were in Babylon. They were true worshipers of Jehovah, and such they resolved to remain.

Daniel and his three friends were rapidly advanced in political power in Babylon (see 2:48-49; 3:30; 5:29; 6:1-3). Daniel's success caused bitter jealousy among the other officials, and a subtle plot was made against him (chap. 6). What a tribute these politicians paid to him when they said: "We shall not find any occasion against this Daniel, except we find it against him concerning the law of his God" (6:5). Vainly they had tried to find some flaw in his government, for they were determined he should not be appointed to the office of ruler over the whole realm. But when they failed, they came to the above conclusion, feeling sure, however, that if they could just raise an issue between King Darius and Jehovah, Daniel would take sides with Jehovah every time, and they could thereby accomplish his defeat. But Daniel could not be defeated as long as he remained true to God. God delivered him from the lions' den, and "Daniel prospered in the reign of Darius, and in the reign of Cyrus the Persian" (6:28).

Daniel served as God's prophet at least until 536 B.C. (10:1).[3] Soon after this he wrote his book, which no doubt was brought back to Jerusalem when the exiles returned to their homeland. The date and circumstances of his death are unknown.

D. Mission

The prominent aspects of Daniel's mission have been already discussed under *Historical Setting*. There it was shown that Daniel's mission was:

1. to Gentiles of Babylon and to Jews in exile
2. concerning Gentile nations and Israel
3. with respect to the succeeding centuries, leading up to the end times

Daniel was a unique prophet among the prophets for various reasons, some of which are listed here:

1. He may not have had a special call to the prophetic ministry, as did Isaiah and Jeremiah.
2. He was given the prophetic gift but not the prophetic office as such.
3. He served in the courts of kings.
4. He prophesied much about Gentile nations.
5. He was the only Old Testament prophet whose book is classified as apocalyptic.[4]
6. His book is the key to the interpretation of all other biblical prophecies of the last days.

---

3. This dateline in 10:1 probably refers to the third year of Cyrus's rule over Babylon, or 536 B.C. The phrase "the first year of king Cyrus" (1:21) probably has reference to the first year of the Jews' permission to return to Jerusalem. See Charles F. Pfeiffer and Everett F. Harrison, eds., *The Wycliffe Bible Commentary* (Chicago: Moody, 1962), p. 776.
4. The book of Revelation is the New Testament apoclypse. See footnote on p. 56 for a further description of this type of literature.

III. THE BOOK OF DANIEL

A. Authenticity

The Daniel referred to by Ezekiel (Ezek. 14:14, 20; 28:3) and by Jesus (Matt. 24:15; Mark 13:14) is the author of this book. From 7:2 onward the book uses the autobiographical first person and, considering the unity of the book, God's words to Daniel in 12:4 imply authorship of the entire book by Daniel. Liberal critics have denied its genuineness, mainly because of (1) its fantastic miracles (e.g., Daniel's deliverance from the lions); (2) its explicit prophecies (many of which were fulfilled in the centuries before Christ); and (3) *alleged* historical inaccuracies. Despite such objections, the book has endured through the centuries as the true words of the Daniel who lived in the sixth century B.C. The lions have not devoured the book, even as they were unable to devour the man!

B. Place in the Canon

In our English Bibles Daniel appears as the last of the five major prophetical books (Isaiah, Jeremiah, Lamentations, Ezekiel, Daniel). In the Hebrew Bibles, Daniel is not grouped with the prophetical books but appears as a historical book in the Hebrew section called Writings. (The Hebrew Bible sections are Law, Prophets, and Writings.) That it was not included among the prophetical books is explained by the fact that although Daniel had the gift and function of prophet (cf. Matt. 24:15), his position was that of a government official. That his book was placed in the Writings as a historical book can be explained by its content, with its apocalyptic visions of world history.

C. Date Written

Daniel probably wrote his book soon after the last dated event occurred (10:1; 536 B.C.). An approximate date would be 530 B.C., or when the prophet was around ninety years of age.

D. Type of Literature

Daniel is an apocalyptic book, the only Old Testament book so classified. Revelation is the one New Testament apocalypse.[5] The

---

5. Revelation and Daniel are closely related, treating the same great subjects and using many like symbols. Studying the one helps in studying the other. One author has written, "The writer of the Apocalypse [Revelation] and Daniel have all things in common, as though they have been let together into the very arcana of God."

word "apocalypse" in its Greek form is translated as "revelation" in Revelation 1:1. Apocalypse is a revelation, an unveiling of secret purposes of God not known before that unveiling. Those purposes concern particularly world events leading up to the messianic kingdom and the consummation of things at the end of the world. The manner in which these events are unveiled is mainly by visions, where imagery and symbolism appear throughout. In Daniel the word "vision" appears twenty-two times; "visions," ten times.

Usually apocalyptic literature is written as prose, but because so much picture language is involved, the prose at places looks much like poetry. In the *Westminster Study Edition of the Bible*[6] the following portions are printed in poetic verse form: 2:20-23; 4:3, 10-12, 14-17, 34*b*-35; 6:26*b*-27; 7:9-10, 13-14.

One unique feature of Daniel is that the book is written in two languages, Hebrew and Aramaic. These appear in the following order:

Hebrew: 1:1-2:4*a*
Aramaic: 2:4*b*–7:28
Hebrew: 8:1–12:13

Hebrew of course was the native language of the Jews, and Aramaic was the official international language of that day, used mainly in international affairs. The reasons for this language structure will appear in the survey study of the next lesson.

E. Importance of the Book

Daniel's unique contribution to the canon of Scripture is that it gives detailed descriptions of the destinies of Gentile nations under the directive sovereign hand of God. Other prophets of Israel spoke of this, but more sparingly, for their main message concerned their own people. The Holy Spirit inspired Daniel to write more about "world" history.

Because we are living in the last days of the times of the Gentiles, the book of Daniel is extremely important for its prophetic disclosures. On this, Merrill Unger writes:

> The book is the key to all biblical prophecy. Apart from the great eschatological disclosures of this book, the entire prophetic portions of the Word of God must remain sealed. Jesus' great Olivet Discourse (Mt. 24-25; Mk. 13; Lk. 21), as well as 2 Thess. 2 and the entire book of the Revelation, can be unlocked only through an understanding of the prophecies of Daniel. The

6. *Westminister Study Edition of the Bible* (Philadelphia: Westminister, 1948).

great themes of NT prophecy, the manifestation of the Antichrist (the man of sin), the Great Tribulation, the second advent of Messiah, the times of the Gentiles, and the resurrection and judgments are all treated in Daniel.[7]

In the next lesson we shall begin our study of the text of Daniel, looking first at the book as a whole, in survey study. As a closing exercise for this lesson, try to answer the following questions about the book's background.

1. What does the Hebrew name "Daniel" mean?

_____

2. God sent Daniel to Babylon to teach Gentile kings what great truth?

_____

_____

_____

3. Name at least seven good qualities of Daniel's character.

_____

_____

_____

4. Describe the times in which Daniel lived.

_____

_____

5. What is meant by "the times of the Gentiles"?

_____

_____

When did this epoch begin?

_____

When will it end?

_____

6. Evaluate Daniel's political career in Babylon.

_____

_____

_____

7. Merrill F. Unger, *Unger's Bible Handbook* (Chicago: Moody, 1966), p. 382.

7. What was one object God had in sending the Jews into captivity?

_____

_____

8. How did God prove His superiority over idols at this time?

_____

_____

_____

9. What is meant by the word "apocalyptic"?

_____

What are the main purposes of apocalyptic writings?

_____

_____

_____

10. What are the main values of the book of Daniel?

_____

_____

_____

Lesson 7

Survey of the Book of Daniel

In the last lesson we studied about the book of Daniel; now we begin the study of the text itself. There is no substitute for one's own personal examination of the Bible text. In this lesson your reading will be of the survey type, looking at the book as a whole. In the lessons that follow, your studies will concentrate on analyzing smaller parts of the book. In either kind of study, a careful and prayerful approach, with observing eyes and an open mind, will bring many rewards to you.

I. OBSERVATION

Let us remind ourselves of the correct order of Bible study: observation first; then interpretation; then application. It is important in Bible study not to seek the meaning of the text (interpretation) until one has carefully observed what the text says (observation). Actually, most interpretations are derived in the analysis stage. In this lesson we are in the survey stage, where only a few interpretations will be sought.

Below are listed some suggestions for your survey of Daniel. Follow them carefully, and be willing to devote much time to this study.

1. First scan the book in one sitting, aloud if possible. Record at least five of your impressions of this book, coming from this reading. Did any words or phrases stand out?

2. Now read through the book a second time, chapter by chapter, seeking a title for each chapter. Record these titles on Chart M. These titles will serve to remind you of the general contents of the book.

3. Look at the first verses of each chapter, noting the references to the kings. These date the events and visions of Daniel. Record this on Chart M. (Review the reigns of the kings as shown on Chart L.)

KINGS

4. What chapters mainly record narrative?

_____

What chapters mainly record visions?

_____

With these observations, begin to develop your own survey chart, like the one worked up in your study of Ezekiel.
5. How is chapter 1 an introductory chapter to the whole book?

_____

Does the last chapter seem to be a unit by itself, or does it continue the vision of chapter 11?

_____

How is the last verse of Daniel a concluding verse to the entire book?

_____

_____

6. Who is the interpreter of the dreams in chapters 1–6?

_____

Who is the interpreter of the dreams in chapter 7–12?

_____

_____

7. Compare Nebuchadnezzar's dream of chapter 2 with Daniel's vision of chapter 7.

_____

_____

_____

8. Observe how most of the visions of the book of Daniel concern Gentile nations. Read chapter 9 again and observe whether this vision is about Gentiles or about Israel.

9. Continue this survey study, recording observations on your chart involving such things as relations, emphases, progression, and turning point. Does there seem to be a unity about the book? Choose a key verse for the book, and from this derive a title.

10. Now study Chart N and the notes given for it.

Notes for Chart N

1. The top of the chart shows how the book may be divided into two equal parts. Also shown here is the chronological progression of kings, in two sequences:

Nebuchadnezzar—Belshazzar—Darius

Belshazzar—Darius—Cyrus

This "backtracking" on the part of the writer is for topical purposes. Note how it fits in with the two-division outline shown above.

2. The bottom of the chart shows an outline suggested by the two languages used in the original text. Such an outline is not apparent to the reader of the English Bible.[1] In your survey reading you were not asked to look for this, even though mention was made of it in previous lesson. (The one reference at 2:4a to "in Syriac [Aramaic]" is not enough information to the English reader concerning this outline.)

Here is what is involved in this structure:

a. From 1:1 to 2:4a, Daniel wrote in Hebrew, the language of the Jews.[2]

b. From 2:4b to 7:28, Daniel wrote in Aramaic, the official language of diplomatic discourse in that day.

c. From 8:1 to the end of the book, Daniel wrote in Hebrew again.

The vital question is, Why did Daniel compose his book this way? The best explanation is that in the two Hebrew sections the Jews are prominent, so the message is in their language; in the Aramaic section the Gentile nations are prominent, so the prophetic decrees are delivered to them, as it were, in the official

---

1. This linguistic structure of Daniel is fully described by Robert D. Culver in his commentary in Charles F. Pfeiffer and Everett F. Harrison, eds., *The Wycliffe Bible Commentary* (Chicago: Moody, 1962), and in his book *Daniel and the Latter Days* (Chicago: Moody, 1954).
2. It may be observed here that Hebrew as the Jews' vernacular began to disappear during the exile years, though it has always remained as the language of the Jews' religion.

SURVEY CHART OF DANIEL

DANIEL

GOD RULES THE WORLD

A KEY VERSE: 4:17

INTRODUCTION	MAINLY HISTORICAL: 6 HISTORICAL NARRATIVES			MAINLY PREDICTIVE: 4 APOCALYTPIC VISIONS		
	Daniel interprets others' dreams			Angel interprets Daniel's dreams		
	Nebuchadnezzar	Bel-shazzar	Darius	Belshazzar	Darius	Cyrus
1	2 3 4 5 6	7	8	9 10	11	12

NEBUCHADNEZZAR'S DREAM —MAN—

DANIEL'S VISION —4 BEASTS—

written in Hebrew	written in Aramaic	written in Hebrew
INTRODUCTION	GENTILE NATIONS	HEBREW NATION
Jews in a Gentile Setting	IMPOTENT IN OPPOSING GOD	—Destiny in God's Plan —Blessed for Obeying God through all the ages to the end of time
	Destinies in God's Hand (2) ... Destinies in God's Hand (7)	centuries before CHRIST

diplomatic language of the world. The survey chart shows the two main sections thus:[3]

Chapters 2-7: GENTILE NATIONS
Chapters 8-12: HEBREW NATION

The introductory chapter 1 involves the Gentile setting, but the spotlight is on the four Jewish boys in that setting. Gentile nations appear much in chapter 8-12 but only as the setting for the experiences of Israel up to the end times.

II. INTERPRETATIONS

On the basis of your study thus far, you have been able to arrive at a few interpretations and conclusions. Consider the following:

1. What appears to be the main theme of the book? Can you think of any supporting themes as well?

_____

_____

_____

2. What do the prophecies reveal concerning the relations between Gentile nations and Israel?

_____

_____

3. How is God shown in this book to be the God of all history?

_____

_____

_____

Further interpretations will be made in the analytical studies of the next lessons.

III. APPLICATIONS

A. Did you notice in your survey study that there are many devotional passages in this book? Make a list of these, writing down the

---

3. The Gentile section here is made to begin at 2:1. Actually, Daniel began writing in Aramaic at 2:4*b* to emphasize the change at the natural point. The spirit of 2:1-4*a* brings those verses into this Gentile section.

truths taught. (Here are some such passages: 1:1-21; 2:20-23; 3:15-25; 6:10-28; 9:3-19.)

_____

_____

_____

_____

_____

B. What are the major doctrines taught by Daniel? For example, what is taught about God?

_____

_____

_____

_____

_____

An interesting observation is Daniel's use of the names of God. Throughout the book the double name is *Adonai* (supreme, sovereign Lord) *Elohim* (mighty God). Only in chapter 9 does the name appear as *Jehovah* (covenant Maker and Fulfiller), where it is used seven times. Read chapter 9 again and account for this name in this setting.

By now you should have a good overall picture of the book of Daniel, including the background of its writing. This is the best preparation for approaching any one part of the book and analayzing its text more thoroughly. The next lesson begins such analysis study.

Lesson 8

Daniel and
His Three Companions

No opening chapter of a book of the Bible introduces its writer in a more fascinating way than does Daniel's. In its narrative are vivid scenes, interesting people, diverse actions, and innumerable spiritual lessons. The chapter is an appropriate introduction to the entire prophecy of Daniel. Your analysis of its twenty-one verses should prove inspiring and fruitful.

I. ANALYSIS

Observe on Chart O how this study segment, one chapter, may be divided into five paragraphs. Mark these divisions in your Bible before you read the chapter. In all of your analytical studies be conscious of the paragraph-by-paragraph movement of the text. The biblical authors did not compose their works haphazardly; each sentence and paragraph unit is where it is for a specific function, serving the larger unit in which it appears.

Read the chapter at least twice before recording any observations on paper. Always keep pencil in hand while reading the Bible text, marking your Bible as you read.

Follow the analysis procedures suggested in the analytical lessons on Ezekiel. For this lesson it is recommended that you record observations on a work sheet similar to analytical Chart O. Some observations are shown as examples. Complete your own personal study before you look too closely at the examples shown. Suggestions for analysis are as follows:

1. What is the main point of each paragraph? Record a paragraph title in the upper right-hand corner of each box.
2. Observe references to God's part in the narrative. Derive spiritual lessons from this.
3. The chapter opens with a reference to the first siege of Jerusalem and closes with a reference to the time of the permission

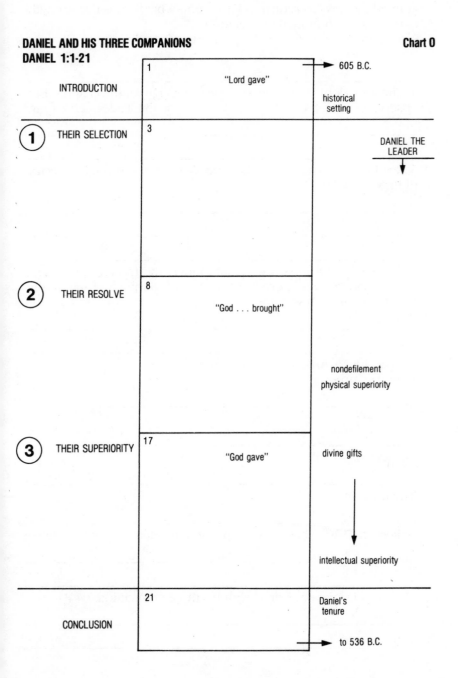

DANIEL AND HIS THREE COMPANIONS   **Chart O**
DANIEL 1:1-21

INTRODUCTION   1   "Lord gave"   605 B.C.

historical setting

(1) THEIR SELECTION   3   DANIEL THE LEADER

(2) THEIR RESOLVE   8   "God . . . brought"

nondefilement
physical superiority

(3) THEIR SUPERIORITY   17   "God gave"   divine gifts

intellectual superiority

CONCLUSION   21   Daniel's tenure

to 536 B.C.

69

granted the Jews to return to Jerusalem. What then is the strength of the word "continued" in verse 21?

Also, how is the chapter on appropriate introduction to Daniel's book?

_____

4. The four Hebrew teenagers appear throughout the chapter. But observe in what ways Daniel is shown to be the leader of the four.

_____

_____

5. Read 1:1-2. What is taught here about God as sovereign Director of history?

_____

_____

_____

6. Read 1:3-7. Observe the qualifications; the training proposed; and the provisions offered. What was the purpose of giving the four young men new names?

_____

_____

7. Read 1:8-16. Analyze the following:
Daniel's purpose:

_____

God's help:

_____

Daniel's proposal:

_____

The outcome:

_____

8. Read 1:17-20. What does the paragraph teach about God's gifts?

_____

_____

How was Daniel compared with his three companions?

_____

_____

How were the four men compared with the enchanters?

9. List some of the major spiritual lessons taught by this opening chapter of Daniel.

_____

_____

_____

II. COMMENTS

1. In the two opening verses of this chapter we are informed, first, as to the condition of the Jews—completely subject to the rule of the Gentiles: second, as to the source of Gentile power (see first sentence of verse 2); and third, as to the heathen estimate of holy things—to be dedicated to their idols.

2. The heathen names. All four names given the Hebrew lads were heathen names, intended to magnify the heathen idols. *The Wycliffe Bible Commentary* lists these meanings:

Hebrew Name	Meaning	Babylonian Name	Meaning
Daniel	God's prince (or judge)	Belteshazzar	Bel's prince
Hananiah	Mercy of Yahweh	Shadrach	Command of Aku (moon-god)
Mishael	Who is what God is?	Meshach	Who is like Aku?
Azariah	Yahweh will help	Abed-nego	Servant of Nebo

3. Purpose of nondefilement. Daniel's motive was religious, not physical.

> Flesh from the king's table was doubtless slain according to pagan ritual and offered to a god. The Jews were forbidden to eat flesh sacrificed to a pagan god (see Ex. 34:15), for it was "serving other gods" in the public eye. Jews faced this problem whenever they ate out of the homeland (Hos. 9:3, 4; Ezk. 4:13, 14). A similar situation prevailed with regard to the wine. A further problem was that Levitical procedures were not regarded . . . (see Lev. 3:17; 6:26; 17:10-14; 19:26).[1]

1. Charles F. Pfeiffer and Everett F. Harrison, eds., *The Wycliffe Bible Commentary* (Chicago: Moody, 1962), p. 775.

The pulse diet which Daniel requested was probably a vegetable diet, which could not be so defiled.

III. SUMMARY

This first chapter of the book of Daniel is a sort of preface to the whole, introducing the reader to the prophet and to the scenes and circumstances of his great prophecies that follow. Three companions are also part of the narrative, but Daniel is the key person. Here is a summary outline of the chapter as it focuses on Daniel:

CAPTURED	to serve a Gentile king	(vv. 1-2)
CHOSEN	according to the king's standards	(vv. 3-7)
TESTED	according to God's standards	(vv. 8-14)
APPROVED	as superior in all respects	(vv. 15-20)
SERVED	to magnify the true God	(v. 21)

Lesson 9

Nebuchadnezzar's Dream and Daniel's Vision

Nebuchadnezzar's dream was the occasion for Daniel's first great prophecy, known as the "ABC of prophecy." This prophecy is basal, being an outline that the later prophecies of Daniel enlarge and which they explain. Nebuchadnezzar, who had so recently been raised to the position of master of the world (politically, at least), lay thinking anxiously one night about his newly acquired possessions, when God was pleased to give him in a dream a prophetic outline of the future of the world powers. About fifty years later Daniel had a vision (also called a dream, 7:1) concerning the same world powers (chap. 7). Because of the similarity of both dreams, they are studied together in this lesson. Review Chart N and note that chapters 2 and 7 begin and conclude the large section called GENTILE NATIONS.

Note: Due to the limitation of space, this manual can only refer to highlights of the passages being studied. Do not let this detract from the necessity of thorough analysis of the various segments of Daniel.

I. ANALYSIS

First read both chapters 2 and 7 for general impressions, noticing the organization of the chapters as shown by the following outlines:

Nebuchadnezzar's Dream		Daniel's Dream	
A. The setting	(2:1-30)	A. The setting	(7:1)
B. The dream	(2:31-35)	B. The dream	(7:2-14, 21-22)
C. The interpretation	(2:36-45)	C. The interpretation	(7:15-20, 23-27)
D. The effect	(2:46-49)	D. The effect	(7:28)

A. Setting of King's Dream

Analyze the setting of Nebuchadnezzar's dream (2:1-30) carefully. Suggestions for study are as follows:
1. Observe how the king's spirit was first troubled (2:1), then angry and furious (2:12). Concerning the first attitude: Had the king completely forgotten what the dream was about? Note: "The thing is gone from me" (2:5b) more accurately reads "The word is certain with me," translated in the *Berkeley Version* as "This word I speak, I mean!" Note how the words "dream" and "interpretation" are used in these other verses: 6, 7, 9, 16, 24-26, 30-35, 36. It may appear from some of these verses that a distinction is made between the dream and the interpretation. However, read 4:5-18 for a similar situation, and note that although the king requested that the dream and the interpretation be told (4:9), the king himself went on to relate the dream (4:10-17).
2. How did Daniel react to the decree of verse 13 (see 2:14-18)?

On what basis was revelation sought from God?

Study carefully the wonderful prayer of verses 20-23. Compare these passages: 9:3-19; 6:9-11; 10:2-12.
3. Observe in 2:25-30 how careful Daniel was to give all glory to God.

B. Comparison of Two Dreams

Let us now compare the two prophetic dreams. For each dream the Bible provides the basic *interpretations.* Identifying the *fulfillment* of the predictions has been the Bible student's task down through the ages. Most scholars admit that the task is a difficult one. The help of commentaries for these chapters is recommended. Chart P will also serve as a study aid.

Use Chart P as a pattern for a work sheet to record your own observations. The chart has intentionally omitted many items, to encourage you to record such observations. After you have completed this, follow these study suggestions:

DREAMS OF THE IMAGE AND FOUR BEASTS
CHAPTERS 2 and 7

Chart P

NEBUCHADNEZZAR'S DREAM OF THE IMAGE		FULFILLMENT	DANIEL'S VISION OF THE FOUR BEASTS	
PROPHECY			**PROPHECY**	
DREAM 2:31-35	INTERPRETATION 2:36-45 →	WORLD POWERS	INTERPRETATION 7:15-28 →	DREAM 7:1-14
① HEAD		NEO-BABYLONIAN 612-539 B.C.		LION ①
② BREASTS AND ARMS		MEDO-PERSIAN 539-331 B.C.		BEAR ②
③ BELLY AND THIGHS		GRECIAN 331-63 B.C.		LEOPARD ③
④ LEGS		ROMAN —3 PERIODS		DIVERSE BEAST ④
		① Supremacy of Ancient Rome 63 B.C.—A.D. 476		
		② Rome-derived governments		10 HORNS
		③ Antichrist		LITTLE HORN
		CONSUMMATION		
GOD'S INDESTRUCTIBLE KINGDOM 2:44		MESSIANIC KINGDOM		ANCIENT OF DAYS (God) on the throne
STONE		CHRIST		SON OF MAN (Christ) given dominion

75

1. Observe how the metals identified with the Gentile powers pro-·
gressively increase in strength. Is there any progression in the
beasts?

_____

_____

2. Keep in mind that not every detail of a symbol is intended to be
interpreted specifically. In the study of apocalyptic literature look
first for the big truths; then move on to the smaller items.
3. The FULFILLMENT column is a widely accepted conservative·
system of interpretation of these chapters. (See also COMMENTS
section.) The identification of Antichrist as the little horn is based
on New Testament passages referring to these last times. (Read 2
Thess. 2:3-10; Rev. 11:2; 13:2, 5-10, 15-17; 19:20.)[1] Since the eschatological approach of this study manual follows the premillennial,
pretribulation system, Chart Q of that system is given here for
orientation:

PREMILLENNIAL SCHEME OF WORLD EVENTS   **Chart Q**

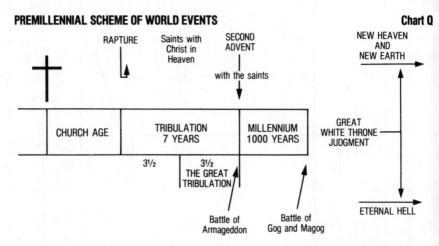

4. Try to see in each symbol of the four kingdoms at least one intended *description* of each kingdom. For example, the twofold
reference of breasts and arms (2:32) suggests a twofold kingdom
(Medo-Persian).

---

1. Read Charles F. Pfeiffer and Everett F. Harrison, eds.; *The Wycliffe Bible Commentary* (Chicago: Moody, 1962), pp. 790-91, for further light on this subject.

5. Observe how a much greater proportion of the text is devoted to the last parts of the visions, involving the final consummation. What does this emphasis teach?

_____

_____

6. Identify the "stone," the "Ancient of days," and the "Son of man."

_____

_____

_____

What advent of Christ is mostly in view in these visions, the first advent or the second? Justify your answer.

_____

_____

7. Write a list of ten major truths taught by these passages.

_____

_____

_____

_____

_____

8. Compare the two effects of the two dreams, as recorded in 2:46-49 and 7:28.

_____

II. COMMENTS

Daniel told Nebuchadnezzar that the meaning of the king's vision was that the God of heaven had given the dominion of the world to Gentile nations; that four of these Gentile powers would successively rise and govern the world; and that in the time of the fourth power, God Himself would set up a kingdom that would crush all the others and endure forever. Daniel identified the first of these four kingdoms to be Nebuchadnezzar's (2:38*b*). Subsequent chapters, verified by secular history, show that these four empires, symbolized in the image by the different materials, were:

first, the Neo-Babylonian (2:38); second, the Medo-Persian (5:28); world power referred to in Luke 2:1). Daniel lived to see the second of these empires come into power; the Old Testament closed while the third was ruling; and at the beginning of the New Testament, the fourth—the Roman—governed the world.

This experience of Nebuchadnezzar afforded a magnificent revelation of God's wisdom, foreknowledge, and power and ought to have been sufficient to cause the king to surrender absolutely to God. But observe Nebuchadnezzar's attitude. He fell on his face before *Daniel*, and worshiped *Daniel*, and made *Daniel* a great man in the kingdom. Although he acknowledged that Jehovah was a "God of gods, and a Lord of kings" (2:47), he did not accept Him as *his* God but referred to Him as *Daniel's* God.

Daniel's vision of the four beasts (chap. 7) referred to the same powers as did Nebuchadnezzar's dream of the human image. More is written of the fourth part of Daniel's vision (fourth beast), which symbolized the Roman Empire, than of any other, because it was during the reign of the fourth Gentile power that God was to set up His kingdom. Verse 24 and 25 of this chapter explain that the little horn of verse 8 is the last king of this last world power and, therefore, the last "king" of Gentile dominion. It is thought by many that this last ruler is to be the Antichrist, that incarnation of Satan whom Christ at His second coming shall destroy (cf. Rev. 13, 17; 2 Thess. 2:3-10). In the midst of the reign of Antichrist, who is designated in all these chapters as "speaking great words against the Most High," the Son of Man receives the kingdom from His Father (see Dan. 7:8-14; 23-27). It is well to read the book of Revelation in connection with the book of Daniel, as they are closely related. The Roman Empire intended by this vision really includes three periods:[2]

1. supremacy of ancient Rome (63 B.C.–A.D. 476)

2. powers derived from that ancient kingdom, up to the end times (period of the ten horns, 7:7)

3. the reign of Antichrist (period of the little horn, 7:8)

III. SUMMARY

As a summary exercise, list the main courses of world history from the beginning of the times of the Gentiles until the commencement of God's eternal kingdom.

2. See Edward J. Young, *The Prophecy of Daniel* (Grand Rapids: Eerdmans, 1949), pp. 149-50.

Lesson 10

Manifestations of Israel's God to Gentile Nations

Some of the Bible's most miraculous and famous events are re-corded in the four chapters of this lesson. These miraculous events demonstrated to the Gentile nations that they were impor-tant in opposing God and that, although Israel as a nation had dis-solved in exile, God was protecting and preserving a remnant of faithful Jews.

I. ANALYSIS

Study each chapter individually, but also look for common themes that unify the stories in this Gentile section. The three subjects to look especially for are: (1) attributes of God, (2) hearts of the Gentiles, (3) virtues of the Jewish young men.

Record your observations on a work sheet of four blocks, as shown in the diagram of Chart R.

Use the paragraph divisions shown. Secure your own out-lines of each chapter, and compare them with the examples given. You will find this to be an interesting exercise.

Give a title to each chapter. Let the title reflect the main theme of the chapter.

Record key words and phrases on the work sheet. Show relat-ed items by using arrows.

Here are some questions regarding each chapter:

A. Chapter 3

Make studies of these topics in the chapter:
  worship: true and false
  faith: concerning this life and the life to come
  opposition of the world:
  divine deliverance:

Chapter 3
GOD THE DELIVERER
—of true worshipers

Situation	1
Accusation	8
Response	13
Test	19
Results	26
	30

Chapter 5
GOD THE JUDGE

Setting	1
Characters	10
	13
	17
Interpretation	24
Results	29
	31

Chapter 4
GOD THE RULER

Salutation	1
Dream	4
Interpretation	19
Fulfillment	28
Response	34
	37

Chapter 6
GOD THE DELIVERER
—of faithful people who pray

DANIEL promoted	1
envied	4
tried	10
delivered	18
	25
Daniel's God glorified	28

miracle: definition, purposes

impersonal recognition of God (vv. 28-29):

B. Chapter 4

Study the chapter in the light of verses 17 and 26. Verse 17 could be considered a key verse for the entire book of Daniel. Concerning God the Ruler, read Isaiah 40:15; Proverbs 21:1; Acts 17:24-26; Romans 13:1.

This chapter consists of a royal letter to the people of Nebuchadnezzar's empire. Note the use of the first person until verse 18, resumed at verse 34. Compare the salutation (vv. 1-3) with the last paragraph (vv. 34-37). Compare Nebuchadnezzar's heart here with that revealed by 3:28-30. What does this chapter teach about:

Influence of a ruler

_____

_____

Pride and presumption

_____

_____

Beneficent effects of a repentant heart

_____

_____

Grace of God

_____

_____

Praise by a restored soul

_____

_____

C. Chapter 5

The feast of this chapter took place on the eve of the fall of Babylon (539 B.C.). (See COMMENTS below.) Daniel, whom Belshazzar did not know until his queen mother talked of him, was now about eighty years old.

1. Note that Daniel's good reputation had remained unmarred through sixty years of service in the palace (5:11-16). Observe also

that Daniel, even in old age, was fearless in exposing the sins of the king.

2. The key of this chapter is the interpretation of the handwriting on the wall. God here is revealed as the supreme Judge. Identify the truths taught about this.

3. Note the suddenness of judgment upon Belshazzar (v. 30.) What does this chapter teach about judgment?

4. Note that Daniel was made "third ruler" in the kingdom (v. 29). Refer to Chart L. Who were the other two contemporary rulers of Babylon, serving at this time, for the few hours before Belshazzar's death?

5. For prophecies that had been made earlier concerning Babylon's fall, read Jeremiah 50-51; Isaiah 44:24-28; 45:1-25.

D. Chapter 6

Darius the Mede recognized the honor granted Daniel by Belshazzar (5:29) and made him the supreme overseer of all his assistants, "But in Daniel's very prominence lay his peril, because of the envy and jealousy of others."[1]

1. Compare the beginning and end of the chapter, as to Daniel's position.

2. Observe references to Daniel's faithful attendance to true Israelitish worship. This is a shining example of God's preservation of a believing remnant of Israel during the captivity years.

3. List the many lessons taught about prayer here.

---

1. Charles F. Pfeiffer and Everett F. Harrison, eds., *The Wycliffe Bible Commentary* (Chicago: Moody, 1962), p. 787.

4. What may have been Daniel's prayer requests, and how were they answered?

_____

_____

_____

_____

5. What is a miracle, and what are the purposes of a miracle?

_____

_____

_____

Observe the effect on Darius of this extraordinary deliverance of Daniel. Note his reference to God's kingdom ("his kingdom") in verse 26.
6. Compare Darius's words of verses 16 and 20.

_____

_____

_____

II. COMMENTS

God bestowed upon Nebuchadnezzar the great gift of world supremacy. Instead of being humbly thankful and obedient to God, we see him in chapter 3 using the imperial power God had given him to set up universal idolatry in the world (3:1-7). When God again displayed His wondrous power in protecting the Hebrews from the flames (3:8-25), Nebuchadnezzar at least acknowledged Jehovah to be the "most high God." He said, "There is no other God that can deliver after this sort," and made a proclamation that no one should speak against this God under penalty of death (3:16-29). There is, however, no hint that he had any intention of *personally* serving the God of Shadrach, Meshach, and Abed-nego.

Nebuchadnezzar had to pass through the terrible experience of chapter 4 before he would "praise and extol and honour the King of heaven." When he did yield, see the magnificent conception that he got of God (4:34-37), and notice that he confessed his own sin and the glory of God throughout his whole domain (4:1-3).

Nebuchadnezzar's particular sin had been the worship of self, but his last successor on the throne of Babylon went much further. Belshazzar not only worshiped himself but added to this

83

the sins of sacrilege (5:1-4), stubbornness (5:22), and impious defiance of God (5:23), with the result stated in the last two verses of chapter 5. Thus the Babylonian Empire (the first of the four great powers symbolized in Nebuchadnezzar's vision) ended in failure and ruin.

The second power, the Medo-Persian, did no better, as is shown in Daniel 6. Here Darius, though a far better man than either Nebuchadnezzar or Belshazzar, allowed himself to be put in the place of God (vv. 6-9), and the spirit of self-worship brought his kingdom to an end. The same thing happened to the other two powers that followed.

Thus Gentiles as well as Jews have proved to be both unworthy and incapable of universal rule. Only the kingdom that God shall set up one day shall be worthy and able to endure forever.

III. SUMMARY

In our study of these four chapters we have seen (1) God revealed as Deliverer, Ruler, and Judge; (2) Gentile nations, whose destinies are in God's hand, impotent in opposing God; (3) devout Jews, preserved throughout the trials and temptations of an alien setting, confirming God's preservation of a faithful remnant of Jews during the times of the Gentiles.

The concluding note of each of the four chapters is a bright one, demonstrating that success in the world comes only of heaven's King:

3:30: "Then the king promoted Shadrach, Meshach, and Abed-nego...."

4:37: "Now I Nebuchadnezzar praise and extol and honour the King of heaven...."

5:29: "Daniel ... should be the third ruler in the kingdom."

6:28: "So this Daniel prospered in the reign of Darius, and in the reign of Cyrus the Persian."

Lesson 11 *Daniel 8:1–9:27*

Visions of the Two Beasts and Seventy Weeks

Daniel now changes from Aramaic to the Hebrew language in order to direct his prophecies to the Jews. In chapters 2-7, Daniel used Aramaic to write concerning the fate of *Gentile* nations. Now he uses the Hebrew language, for his prophecies concern mainly the destiny of the *Jewish* nation in a Gentile world.

There are three visions in chapters 8-12: (1) the two beasts (chap. 8); (2) the seventy weeks (chap. 9); (3) the conflicts of kings (chaps. 10-12). This lesson is devoted to the first two. Review Chart N to recall the setting of these visions.

I. ANALYSIS

A. Vision of the Two Beasts (8:1-27)

In this vision Daniel saw two of the Gentile powers (Medo-Persian and Grecian), which he had seen in the visions of chapters 2 and 7. The main purpose of this vision is *Jewish-oriented*: to show that out of the Grecian Empire would arise one who, though a persecutor of God's people for a time, would himself eventually be "broken" (8:25).

For your study of this chapter, follow the procedures suggested in earlier lessons. The outline of the procession of the vision shown in Chart S will help you in your study.

Observe by the outline how the Jews were involved in this prophecy. This is the key to the vision. Antiochus Epiphanes, king of Syria 175-163 B.C., was Israel's archenemy in the centuries before Christ.

> In his attempt to Hellenize the Jews he had a pig sacrificed on the altar in Jerusalem, forbade circumcision, and destroyed all

VISION OF THE TWO BEASTS
DANIEL 8

VISION 8:1-14	INTERPRETATION 8:15-26	FULFILLMENT	
TWO-HORNED RAM (v. 3)	Media and Persia (v. 20)	MEDO-PERSIAN EMPIRE (550-331 B.C.)	
HE-GOAT (v. 5)	Grecia (v. 21)	GRECIAN EMPIRE (331-63 B.C.)	
GREAT HORN (v. 5)	first king (v. 21)	ALEXANDER THE GREAT	
great horn broken	king broken (v. 22)	death of Alexander (323 B.C.)	
FOUR HORNS (v. 8)	4 kingdoms arise (v. 22)	FOUR KINGDOMS: Greece (Macedonia), Thrace, Syria, and Egypt	
LITTLE HORN (v. 9)	king of fierce countenance (v. 23)	ANTIOCHUS EPIPHANES Syrian king	
cast down host (v. 10)	destroy the holy people (v. 24)	JEWS' INVOLVEMENT	persecution of the Jews
daily sacrifice taken away (v. 11)			removal of Temple sacrifices 167 B.C.
2,300 days (v. 14)	many days (v. 26)		173-163 B.C. (reign of Antiochus)
then . . . sanctuary cleansed (v. 14)			temple purified 164 B.C.
	he shall be broken (v. 25)		end of persecutions with Antiochus's death

the OT books he could find. These outrages involved him in the Maccabean war in which the Syrian armies were repeatedly defeated by the brilliant Judas Maccabeus.[1]

The tribulations of the Jews during Antiochus's reign are described in Hebrews 11:34-39. When the Jews were being persecuted by Antiochus, how would this portion of their Scripture have inspired them to persevere? Compare this with the message of Revelation to the Christians of the seven churches undergoing the ordeals of Domitian's persecutions at the end of the first century A.D.

The "little horn" of verse 9 should not be identified as the "little horn" of Daniel 7:8, 24-26, who is the Antichrist of the end time. However, as will be seen in Lesson 12, Antiochus Epiphanes may be said to foreshadow the Antichrist, since both are alike in their idolatry and desecration of the Temple (cf. Matt. 24:15-21; 2 Thess. 2:3-5; Rev. 13:1-18).[2]

B. Vision of the Seventy Weeks (9:1-27)

First read through the chapter for first impressions. Notice the three parts: (1) historical introduction; (2) Daniel's prayer; (3) the vision. Concerning the introduction, what is Daniel's purpose in referring to the seventy-year prophecy (Jer. 25:11-12; 29:10) in this context?

1. Daniel's Prayer (9:3-19). This is a wonderful example of a passionate prayer of confession and intercession. It merits your attention in careful and prayerful analysis. Record your study on an analytical chart, using the following paragraph units: Israel's Sin (vv. 3-11a); The Consequences (vv. 11b-14); The Plea (vv. 15-19). Careful analysis will reveal innumerable precious truths. At the end of your analysis write a list of lessons taught about prayer. Compare these with what is taught about prayer by the following references in other parts of the Bible: Exodus 32:10-14; Psalm 32:5; 51:4; Matthew 6:5-18; 9:27; 15:22; 17:15; 20:30-31; Luke 11:1-13; 18:10-14; 2 Corinthians 12:7-9; James 5:16.

2. The Vision (9:20-27). Observe how the prceeding context (9:1-19) leads up to this vision. Daniel was now thinking, "We have almost fulfilled the seventy-year judgment of exile; what lies in store for us?" (cf. 9:2). So he prayed to God, confessing Israel's sins and asking his merciful God to forgive and restore (9:15-19).

1. Merrill C. Tenney, ed., *The Zondervan Pictorial Bible Dictionary* (Grand Rapids: Zondervan, 1963), p. 48.
2. See Merrill F. Unger, *Unger's Bible Handbook* (Chicago: Moody, 1966), p. 391.

While Daniel was still praying this prayer (9:20-23), the angel Gabriel revealed to him a prophetic outline of Israel's future from then until the end time.

II. OBSERVATIONS

Read the vision (vv. 24-27) a few times before recording your observations. Three kinds of predictions are involved. List, in the space provided, the items under each group:

1. *End results of the period* (9:24)

NEGATIVE	POSITIVE
a. _____	d. _____
b. _____	e. _____
c. _____	f. _____

2. *Breakdown of the seventy-week time reference*
   a. 7 weeks (9:25)
   b. 62 weeks (9:25-26)
   c. 1 week (9:27)
   d. middle of the week (9:27)
3. *Events associated with the periods.*

   a. _____

   b. _____

   c. _____

   d. _____

III. INTERPRETATIONS

Among evangelicals there are two main schools of interpretation of this vision. Both are agreed that the "weeks" of the vision are heptads ("sevens") of years, one week being seven years. One view, referred to by Edward J. Young as the "traditional messianic interpretation,"[3] sees the seventieth week as fulfilled in the first century A.D., without a hiatus of a Church Age. According to this view the prince of verse 26 is Titus, destroyer of the Temple and Jerusalem in A.D. 70; and the "he" of verse 27 is Christ, whose death removed the need for further sacrifices under the old covenant.

3. This is the view held by Edward J. Young, *The Prophecy of Daniel* (Grand Rapids: Eerdmans, 1949).

The other view (the view subscribed to in this manual), recognizing a gap between the sixty-ninth and seventieth weeks, sees the vision as an outline of Israel's history up to the great Tribulation of end times.[4] This is diagrammed in Chart T.

SEVENTIETH WEEK OF DANIEL

Chart T

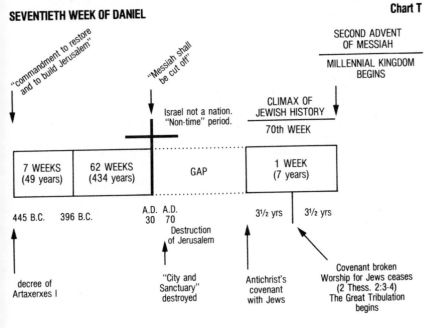

Study the chart in connection with the text of Daniel 9:24-27. Robert D. Culver gives the following reasons for holding to a time gap in this vision:[5]

1. Jesus placed the culminating week with its "abomination" in the times of the final Antichrist, just before His second advent (Matt. 24:15).
2. Daniel 7:25, parallel to 9:27, is a prophecy of the times of the final Antichrist.
3. The period of three and one-half times or years is always mentioned in Scripture in an eschatological (end times) setting (Rev. 11:2-3; 12:6, 14).

4. Unger., *op. cit.*, and Robert D. Culver, in his commentary in Charles F. Pfeiffer and Everett F. Harrison, eds., *The Wycliffe Bible Commentary* (Chicago: Moody, 1962), present this view, which is the view of many premillennial scholars.
5. Cited in Pfeiffer and Harrison, p. 795.

4. The six things to be accomplished in the seventy weeks (Dan. 9:24) require the second advent of Christ and the restoration and conversion of Israel.

You will want to come to your own conclusions as to whether a time gap is intended by the vision. Refer to the commentaries already cited for further help on the two main views outlined here.

IV. CONCLUSIONS

Go back over both visions of this lesson, and review the main events prophesied concerning Israel, which as of Daniel's day were all still future. Account for Daniel's reactions of 8:27. Considering his prayer of 9:3-19, what items of the vision of the seventy weeks would Daniel have surely understood? How much of this vision do you think was intended to be understood in Daniel's day, when Gabriel gave it? (Read again 9:23; cf. 10:1 of the next vision.) Do the New Testament and world history shed more light on such Old Testament prophecies than what the prophets and people had in the day the prophecies were first given?

Vision of the Conflicts of Kings

Daniel's final vision revealed to the prophet more of Israel's future, culminating in the messianic kingdom. Parts of the vision had already been seen in earlier visions; other parts were new.

Daniel did not fully understand everything of the visions shown him (cf. 12:8), but he had a spirit and attitude that were acceptable to God. His humility kept him from an intellectual sophistication that demanded a human explanation of all divine revelation. "Daniel was still no expert on prophetic interpretation. There will be no expert until prophecy becomes history."[1] The multifold vision of this lesson contains some difficult portions, as do the earlier visions of the book. In your study, maintain a patient and inquiring spirit, and do not let any difficult detail detract from the clear overall teachings of the vision.

I. ANALYSIS

First, notice the general outline of this section of Daniel. The passage is divided into three parts: (1) prologue (10:1–11:1); (2) the vision (11:2–12:3); (3) epilogue (12:4-13). In the course of your study, add your own observations and outlines to Chart U.

A. Prologue (10:1–11:1)

Compare the vision of the man (10:5 ff.) with the visions of Ezekiel 1 and Revelation 1:13-15. What was God's purpose in giving such *introductory* visions to these men of God?

What do you learn about Daniel from this chapter?

1. Charles F. Pfeiffer and Everett F. Harrison, eds., *The Wycliffe Bible Commentary* (Chicago: Moody, 1962), p. 799.

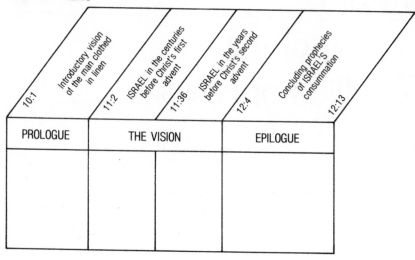

PROLOGUE | THE VISION | EPILOGUE

B. The Vision (11:2–12:3)

The vision may be divided into two parts:

1. Israel in the centuries before Christ's first advent. Here are prophesied events concerning the Grecian period up to Antiochus Epiphanes' persecution of the Jews (11:2-35).

2. Israel in the years before Christ's second advent. Here are prophesied end-time events, with Antichrist as a main character (11:36–12:3). This passage is difficult reading because (1) it is long, (2) very few interpretations are given, and (3) references to Israel or the Holy Land are not always clear. After you have read the passage once, study the following outlines and comments, to give you a bearing in your course. The key here is to see the *big* movements in the vision.

1. Meanings of the Main Symbols.

a. the four kings of Persia (11:2) after Cyrus: Cambyses, Smerdis, Darius Hystaspis, Xerxes

b. "mighty king" of Greece (11:3): Alexander the Great

c. "king of the south" (11:5, *et al.*): king of Egypt (Ptolemaic kingdom)

d. "king of the north" (11:6, *et al.*): king of Syria (Seleucid kingdom)

e. "vile person" (11:21): Antiochus Epiphanes, king of Syria 175-163 B.C.

f. "the holy covenant" (11:28): things involving God's people Israel, including their land

g. "sanctuary of strength" (11:31): the Temple of Jerusalem

h. "the people that do know their God" (11:32): believing Israel in Palestine

i. the willful king (11:36): Antichrist of end times

j. "the indignation be accomplished" (11:36): God's judgment (cf. Isa. 26:20-21)

k. "the time of the end" (11:40): the point of consummation, when the kingdoms of the world, opposing God, will be replaced by the messianic kingdom (cf. 1 Cor. 15:24; Matt. 13:39; 28:20; Rev. 19:11 ff.)

l. "king of the south;" "king of the north" (11:40): two unidentified nations opposing Antichrist; not the kings cited prior to 11:36

m. "the glorious land" (11:41): Palestine

n. "a time of trouble" (12:1): God's chastening of Israel, before their deliverance (12:1*b*)

2. Structure of the Vision. As indicated earlier, the vision is of two parts. The break at verse 36 does not appear at first glance, because the prophetic perspective jumps over a long interval of centuries as though they did not exist.[2]

Now that you have become acquainted with the meanings of the main symbols and with the structure of the vision, read the passage again, letting the big items retain their prominence. Spend most of your time on 11:21–12:3, since Antichrist is the main character of the vision, with reference to the experience of Israel.

An outline of the important section 11:36–12:3 is as follows:

1. Antichrist's character (11:36-39)
2. Antichrist's actions (11:40-45)
3. Israel's trouble (12:1)
4. Israel's deliverance (12:2)
5. Israel's rewards (12:3)

You may want to develop your own outline of this section.

Observe especially the climax of the vision (beginning at 11:45). List the many important events prophesied here. Who of the people of Israel will be saved? (See 12:1*b*.) Read Romans 11 for Paul's inspired commentary on Israel's future.

2. Recall a similar gap of time in the vision of the seventy weeks. There, the gap existed because time was not reckoned while Israel as a *nation* did not exist. Here, the gap exists because the vision moves from the *foreshadowing* of the Antichrist (in Antiochus) to the Antichrist *himself.* Consult Pfeiffer and Harrison, p. 797, for Robert Culver's seven reasons supporting a gap between verses 35 and 36.

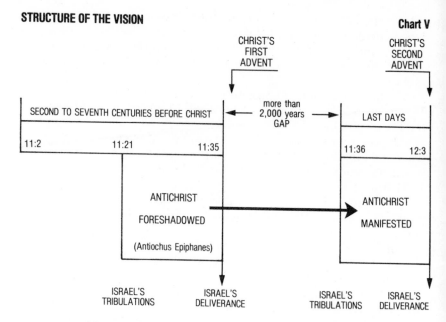

Chart V

C. Epilogue (12:4-13)

The epilogue records reactions of Daniel, final instructions to him, and the additions of a few final prophecies. Concerning the latter, note the time references. The "time, times, and a half" (12:7) are three and one-half years (one plus two plus one-half), the midpoint of Daniel's last week. The 1,290 days of verse 11 are 43 months, or one month beyond the end of three and one-half yeas (42 months); the 1,335 days would extend even further:

ANALYSIS OF "TIME, TIMES, AND A HALF" Chart W

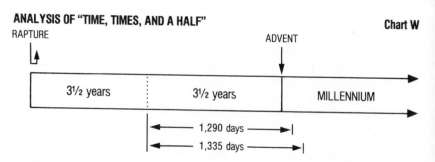

It has been suggested that the extra time is for the initial preliminary work of the Messiah's millennial reign. "The Millennium, if a

true administration of heaven's rule on earth in a visible manner, will require time for administrative processes to begin to work."[3]

II. THE LAST VERSE OF DANIEL

Observe that the last verse of the book of Daniel contains a command and a promise to the prophet. What spiritual lesson for all servants of God is suggested by the command "Go thy way till the end?" When would Daniel rest, and when would he stand? The *Berkeley Version* reads, "But you, go on to the end; you will rest and you will arise for your allotment at the end of time" (12:13). What a grand hope for all God's people!

III. COMPARISONS OF DANIEL'S VISIONS

For a summary exercise, it is profitable to compare the main coverages of Daniel's five visions. The diagram in Chart X will help to show parallels and differences. As you study it, review in your mind the parts of each vision. You will probably want to go back to the lessons of this manual to refresh your memory.

1. Keep in mind that no part of Scripture is superfluous. Whatever God inspired to be written down was of purpose. When repetitions appear, there is a reason.

2. Note how different the first two visions are from the last three. Account for this by referring to the topical outline of the book. (See Chart N, recalling the two sections GENTILE NATIONS and HEBREW NATION.)

3. The four periods of Israel's woes, beginning with captivity, are shown at the bottom of Chart N. Observe that the second and fourth of these are given prominence in the visions. Try to account for this.

_____

_____

4. Recall that kings and kingdoms are prominent in the visions. What symbolic use is made of this in the visions?

_____

_____

3. Pfeiffer and Harrison, p. 799.

COMPARISONS OF DANIEL'S VISIONS

Chart X

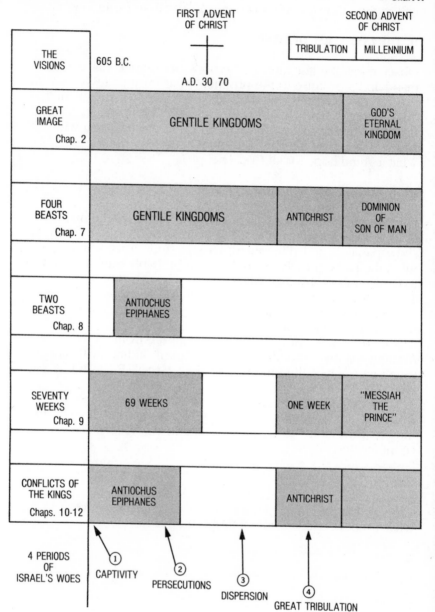

THE VISIONS	605 B.C.	FIRST ADVENT OF CHRIST † A.D. 30 70	SECOND ADVENT OF CHRIST

| | | | | TRIBULATION | MILLENNIUM |

| GREAT IMAGE Chap. 2 | GENTILE KINGDOMS | GOD'S ETERNAL KINGDOM |

| FOUR BEASTS Chap. 7 | GENTILE KINGDOMS | ANTICHRIST | DOMINION OF SON OF MAN |

| TWO BEASTS Chap. 8 | ANTIOCHUS EPIPHANES |

| SEVENTY WEEKS Chap. 9 | 69 WEEKS | ONE WEEK | "MESSIAH THE PRINCE" |

| CONFLICTS OF THE KINGS Chaps. 10-12 | ANTIOCHUS EPIPHANES | ANTICHRIST |

4 PERIODS OF ISRAEL'S WOES

① CAPTIVITY
② PERSECUTIONS
③ DISPERSION
④ GREAT TRIBULATION

96

IV. A CONCLUDING EXERCISE

How has the book of Daniel impressed you? Do you feel you know more about God and His wonderful sovereign ways? Meditate on Paul's exclamation, spoken after his discourse on Israel in Romans 9-11:

> O the depth of the riches
>   both of the wisdom and knowledge of God!
> How unsearchable are his judgments,
>   and his ways past finding out!
> For who hath known the mind of the Lord?
> Or who hath been his counsellor?
> Or who hath first given to him, and it shall be
>   recompensed unto him again?
> For of him, and through him, and to him,
>   are all things:
> To whom be glory for ever.
> Amen.   (Romans 11:33-36)

GEOGRAPHY OF EZEKIEL AND DANIEL

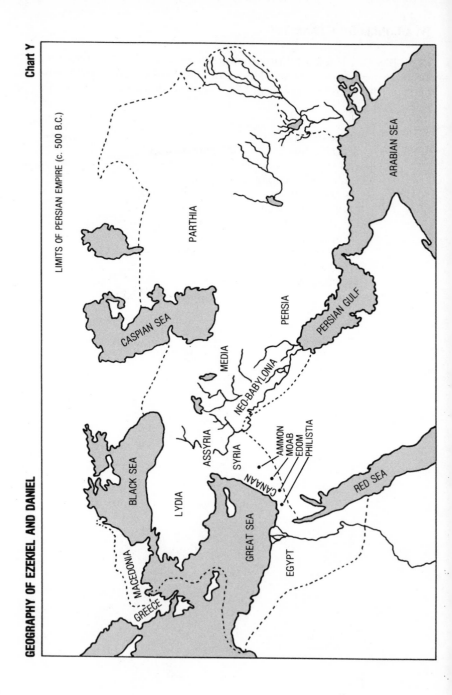

LIMITS OF PERSIAN EMPIRE (c. 500 B.C.)

PARTHIA

CASPIAN SEA

MEDIA

NEO-BABYLONIA

PERSIA

PERSIAN GULF

ARABIAN SEA

ASSYRIA

SYRIA

CANAAN

AMMON
MOAB
EDOM
PHILISTIA

LYDIA

BLACK SEA

MACEDONIA

GREECE

GREAT SEA

EGYPT

RED SEA

	ISAIAH	JEREMIAH	EZEKIEL	DANIEL
KNOWN AS:	The Royal Prophet Evangelical Prophet Messianic Prophet	The Weeping Prophet The Prophet of Judgment	The Prophet of Visions The Prophet of the Exile The Other Son of Man	The Prophet of Gentile Times
PROPHESIED TO:	Jews in Judea	Jews in Judea and in Captivity	Captive Jews in Babylon	Gentile Kings and Captive Jews
CONCERNING:	Judah and Jerusalem, Isa. 1:1; 2:1	Judah and Nations, Jer. 1:5; 9:10; 2:1-2	The Whole House of Israel, Ezek. 2:3-6; 3:4-10, 17	Gentile Nations, Dan. 2:36 ff., and Israel, Dan. 9
DURING REIGNS OF:	Uzziah, Jotham, Ahaz, and Hezekiah, Kings of Judah, Isa. 1:1	Josiah, Jehoahaz, Jehoiakim, Jehoiachin, Zedekiah, Kings of Judah, Jer. 1:2-3	Zedekiah, King of Judah and Nebuchadnezzar, King of Babylon	Jehoiakim, Jehoiachin, and Zedekiah (Kings of Judah), Nebuchadnezzar, Darius, and Cyrus (Gentile Kings)
DATES B.C.:	From 739 to 692	From 627 to 574	From 393 to 559	From 605 to 536
NUMBER OF YEARS HE PROPHESIED:	47	53	34	69
PROPHET'S CALL:	Isa. 6	Jer. 1:4-19	Ezek. 1—3	———
POLITICAL CONDITION:	Judah Menaced by Syria and Israel Alliance with Assyria Assyria Repulsed	Hostilities with Egypt and Babylon Deportation of Captives	Some Jews Captive in Babylon Other Jews Still in Judea Threatened with Captivity	Jews in Babylonian Captivity
RELIGIOUS CONDITION:	Backslidden Hypocritical	Revival Under Josiah Much Sin and Idolatry After Josiah's Death	National Unbelief, Disobedience, and Rebellion	As a Nation Out of Communion with God A Small Believing Remnant
HISTORICAL SETTING:	2 Kings 15—20 2 Chron. 26—30	2 Kings 24—25	Dan. 1—6	Dan. 1—6

Bibliography

SELECTED SOURCES FOR FURTHER STUDY

Barnes, Albert. *Daniel*. Vol. 2. Grand Rapids: Baker, 1950.

Beasley-Murray, G. R. "Ezekiel." In *The New Bible Commentary*, edited by F. Davidson. Grand Rapids: Eerdmans, 1953.

Boutflower, Charles. *In and Around the Book of Daniel*. Grand Rapids: Zondervan, 1963.

Culver, Robert D. *Daniel and the Latter Days*. Chicago: Moody, n.d.

———. "Daniel." In *The Wycliffe Bible Commentary*, edited by Charles F. Pfeiffer and Everett F. Harrison. Chicago: Moody, 1962.

DeHaan, M. R. *Daniel the Prophet*. Grand Rapids: Zondervan, 1947.

Ellison, H. L. *Ezekiel: The Man and His Message*. Grand Rapids: Eerdmans, 1956.

Feinberg, Charles L. *The Prophecy of Ezekiel*. Chicago: Moody, 1969.

Hengstenberg, E. W. *Christology of the Old Testament*. Reprint. Grand Rapids: Kregel, 1970.

Ironside, Henry Allen. *Lectures on Daniel the Prophet*. New York: Loizeaux, 1920.

Jensen, Irving L. *Jensen's Survey of the Old Testament*. Chicago: Moody, 1978.

Johnson, Philip C. *The Book of Daniel*. Grand Rapids: Baker, 1964.

Luck, G. Coleman. *Daniel*. Chicago: Moody, 1958.

Mc Clain, Alva J. *Daniel's Prophecy of the Seventy Weeks*. Grand Rapids: Zondervan, 1940.

Newell, Philip R. *Daniel*. Chicago: Moody, 1962.

Pearson, Penton T. "Ezekiel." In *The Wycliffe bible Commentary*, edited by Charles F. Pfeiffer and Everett F. Harrison, Chicago: Moody, 1962.

Pentecost, J. Dwight. *Prophecy for Today*. Grand Rapids: Zonder-
van, 1961.
Pfeiffer, Charles F. *An Outline of Old Testament History*. Chicago:
Moody, 1960.
Tenney, Merrill C., ed. *The Zondervan Pictorial Bible Dictionary*.
Grand Rapids: Zondervan, 1963.
Walvoord, John F. *Daniel: The Key to Prophetic Revelation*. Chica-
go: Moody, 1971.
_____. *Israel in Prophecy*. Grand Rapids: Zondervan, 1962.
Young, Edward J. "Daniel." In *The New Bible Commentary*, edited
by F. Davidson. Grand Rapids: Eerdmans, 1953.

Moody Press, a ministry of the Moody Bible Institute,
is designed for education, evangelization, and edification.
If we may assist you in knowing more about Christ
and the Christian life, please write us without obligation:
Moody Press, c/o MLM, Chicago, Illinois 60610.